LOGIC PUZZLES

NORMAN D. WILLIS

STERLING

New York / London
www.sterlingpublishing.com

To my fiancée, Eleanor Rogers;
her ideas for puzzle settings,
as well as her quality review,
contributed significantly to this book.

STERLING and the distinctive Sterling logo are registered
trademarks of Sterling Publishing Co., Inc.

Library of Congress Cataloging-in-Publication Data Available

10 9 8 7 6 5 4 3 2 1

Published by Sterling Publishing Company, Inc.
387 Park Avenue South, New York, N.Y. 10016
© 2000, 2008 by Norman D. Willis
Distributed in Canada by Sterling Publishing
c/o Canadian Manda Group, 165 Dufferin Street
Toronto, Ontario, Canada M6K 3H6
Distributed in the United Kingdom by GMC Distribution Services
Castle Place, 166 High Street, Lewes, East Sussex, England BN7 1XU
Distributed in Australia by Capricorn Link (Australia) Pty. Ltd.
P.O. Box 704, Windsor, NSW 2756, Australia

Printed in China
All rights reserved

Sterling ISBN-13: 978-1-4027-5468-5
        ISBN-10: 1-4027-5468-X

For information about custom editions, special sales, premium and
corporate purchases, please contact Sterling Special Sales
Department at 800-805-5489 or specialsales@sterlingpublishing.com.

Contents

2. Who Dunnit?   65

3. Fragments 119

The A's 120

The B's 162

5. Letters for Digits 241

The A's 242

6. Desert Foothills Golf 257

9. The Dragons of Lidd 305

The Dragons from Wonk 317

Before You Begin

Logic puzzles involve the application of deductive reasoning. They are fun because they are challenging and, in addition, they are an excellent means of expanding your mental power. The challenge lies in forming conclusions concerning the information afforded in each puzzle and arriving at the solution. No previous knowledge is required, and the solutions do not depend on memory, wordplay, or deception—only your own ability to reason logically.

In this book, there are nine different kinds of logic puzzles, which have been separated into nine sections. You will find that the puzzles in each section vary in difficulty; generally the easier puzzles will come first in a section, graduating toward the more difficult.

In solving the puzzles, follow a systematic approach, including trial and error. Assume that each alternative provided leads to the correct solution, and look for contradictions. When you have discarded faulty assumptions, what remains is the solution. Resist turning to the puzzle solutions until you feel you have solved the puzzle, or have given it your best effort.

Diagrams are provided for most types of puzzles, to assist you in organizing your conclusions.

1.
Hypotheses

These puzzles contain assumptions that may or may not be valid. To solve them you must differentiate between those that are valid and those that are not valid.

The Voyage of Singood the Sailor

During his growing years, Singood had heard many tales of his illustrious father, Sinbad the Sailor, and his seven voyages during which he was able to amass an enormous fortune. Singood wished to undertake adventures of his own and achieve fabulous wealth, as did his father.

P1-1 A Giant Fish

Singood signed on as a sailor on a merchant ship. After being at sea for several weeks, the ship was blown far off course by a storm and came within sight of what appeared to be an island. The captain and crew, including Singood, attempted to row ashore.

Amazingly, this happened not to be an island but the very same giant fish encountered by Singood's father, Sinbad the Sailor, during the first of his seven voyages at sea. The giant predator's method was to give the appearance of an island in order to engulf any unsuspecting prey that came near. Singood and his fellow sailors sought to escape by swimming back to the ship.

From the statements below, what time of day was it and what was the outcome of the encounter?

1. If the monster fish had just consumed a merchant ship and several whales and was not interested in another meal, then it was evening.
2. If it was morning, the ship and crew were too small to be noticed by the monster.

3. If it was evening, then the monster fish was too old and slow to catch the ship and crew.
4. If the giant fish was too old and slow to catch the crew and ship, then it was morning.

	too small	too slow	not interested
morning			
evening			

Mark a plus (+) or a minus (–) sign as you determine whether or not a statement is valid.

Solution on pages 328–329

P1-2 An Enchanted Island

The ship and crew came within sight of an unknown island. The trees and lovely flowers growing on it convinced them that this time it was really an island.

Singood, the first mate, and the second mate went ashore to explore. Unknown to them the island was enchanted, and the instant the three set foot on land they fell under a spell and lost their memories. They could recall nothing, not even who they were or why they were there.

From the statements below, which one of A, B, and C was Singood, which one was the first mate, and which one was the second mate?

1. If A was Singood, then B was the first mate.
2. If B was not Singood, then C was the first mate.
3. If A was the first mate, then B was the second mate.

	1st mate	2nd mate	Singood
A			
B			
C			

As in the previous puzzle, mark a plus or minus sign as you draw your conclusions.

Solution on page 329

P 1-3 A Third Island

Singood decided to take a swim, and the instant he did his memory returned. He called to his shipmates and they were able to return to their ship.

The ship came within sight of another island just as the adventurers were in need of supplies. As they drew near, the sailors beheld a beautiful sight. Wavy palm trees, a glistening waterfall, a crystal clear lake, and many trees laden with ripe fruit could be clearly seen. The captain chose to be cautious and sent Singood, the first mate, and the second mate toward shore in the ship's dinghy.

In spite of Singood's energetic rowing, the island appeared to remain at the same distance as when they had started off. Then, mysteriously, its features began to disappear bit by bit in front of their eyes. Finally, there was nothing left to see but a barren strip of land, which also slowly faded from sight, leaving the sailors with no trace of the land ever having been there.

From the statements that follow, in what order did the principal island features disappear?

1. If the wavy palms vanished first, then the fruit trees vanished third.

2. If the fruit trees vanished third, the waterfall vanished first.
3. If the waterfall vanished first, then the clear lake vanished fourth.
4. If the clear lake vanished fourth, then the fruit trees vanished first.
5. The clear lake vanished first unless either the waterfall or the wavy palms vanished first.
6. If the clear lake vanished first, neither the fruit trees nor the waterfall vanished fourth.

	1st	2nd	3rd	4th
clear lake				
fruit trees				
waterfall				
wavy palms				

Solution on page 330

P1-4 Return to the Ship

When the three sailors turned back toward their ship, they found it as only a distant speck on the horizon. Realizing that Singood was tired from rowing, they decided to take turns at the task of returning to their ship.

From the statements below, what was the order in which they rowed back to the ship?

1. If Singood was not the first to take a turn rowing, then he was the third to take a turn.
2. If the first mate was first to take a turn rowing, then the second mate was second to take a turn.
3. If the second mate was second to take a turn rowing, then the first mate was third to take a turn.
4. If the first mate was third to take a turn rowing, then Singood was second to take a turn.

	1st mate	2nd mate	Singood
1st turn			
2nd turn			
3rd turn			

Solution on pages 331–332

P1-5 A Gigantic Bird

The three sailors rowed their boat toward the ship, but before they were even halfway there, a gigantic bird swooped down on them and plucked them up. They were carried to a distant land, where they were deposited in a nest high in a tree.

From the statements that follow, what was the wingspan of the gigantic bird and how far did it carry the three sailors?

1. If the wingspan of the gigantic bird was either 20 or 30 meters wide, it carried the three sailors for 50 leagues.
2. If the gigantic bird carried the three shipmates 75 leagues, its wingspan was not 40 or 50 meters wide.
3. If the wingspan of the gigantic bird was 40 or 50 meters wide, it carried the three sailors 75 leagues.
4. If the gigantic bird's wingspan was not 40 or 50 meters wide, then it was 20 or 30 meters wide.

	20–30 m.	40–50 m.
50 leagues		
75 leagues		

Solution on page 332

P1-6 Attacked by a Giant Serpent

After the gigantic bird deposited Singood, the first mate, and the second mate high in a tree, one of the three scrambled to the ground. He was immediately attacked by a giant serpent.

A second of the three hurried to the rescue, and the two sailors managed to discourage the serpent long enough that they were able to retreat safely back into the tree.

Which one of the three sailors was attacked by the serpent, which one came to the rescue, and which one remained in the tree?

1. If Singood was attacked by the serpent, then the first mate stayed in the tree.
2. If the first mate stayed in the tree, the second mate did not go to the rescue.
3. If the second mate did not stay in the tree, the first mate was attacked by the serpent.
4. If Singood stayed in the tree, the first mate went to the rescue.

	attacked	to rescue	stayed
Singood			
1st mate			
2nd mate			

Solution on page 333

P1-7 Captured by the One-Eyed Giant

After the serpent left, the three shipmates began to make their way back to the ship. They hadn't gone far, however, when a storm came up. Seeking refuge in a large cave, they were captured by a manlike creature of enormous size, with only one eye. He deposited them in a corner of the cave, next to a pile of bones. It was apparent that they were to become meals for the giant, if nothing were done.

While the giant slept, blocking the cave entrance with his massive body, the sailors discussed how to escape. Each one had an idea. The three possibilities were: attempt to climb over the giant while he was still sleeping; hide under the pile of bones until the giant left the cave; or sharpen a large stick and stab the giant in the single eye.

From the statements that follow, which shipmate arrived at which idea?

1. If Singood's idea was to stab the giant in the eye, then the second mate's idea was not to hide under the pile of bones.

2. If the first mate's idea was to stab the giant in the eye, or hide under the bones, then Singood's idea was to climb over the sleeping giant.
3. If Singood's idea was to climb over the giant, or to hide under the bones, then the first mate's idea was to stab the giant in the eye.

	climb over	stab giant	under bones
Singood			
1st mate			
2nd mate			

Solution on page 334

P1-8 Escape from the Giant

Held captive in the cave by a one-eyed giant, Singood, the first mate, and the second mate considered their options—and did manage to make their escape. The sailors then proceeded on a long journey, which took either two or three months, back to the sea, where they had left their ship.

Which escape idea did they undertake and how long did the return to the sea take?

1. If the journey took two months, then the three sailors escaped by hiding under a pile of bones.
2. If the journey took three months, then the sailors escaped from the giant by climbing over him while he was asleep.
3. If the sailors escaped from the giant by climbing over him while he was asleep, then the journey took two months.
4. If the sailors did not escape from the giant by stabbing him with a sharpened stick, then the journey took either two or three months.

	climb over	under bones	stab giant
2 months			
3 months			

Solution on page 335

P1-9 An Attack by Giant Spiders

At one point during their long trek to the sea, the three sailors suddenly found themselves under attack by three giant spiders that quickly surrounded them. Taking advantage of the many stones lying about, the sailors quickly began throwing them at the spiders. Each sailor singled out a spider and hurled stones with telling accuracy.

Although the spiders were huge and fierce-looking, with long, menacing-looking legs, they were no match for the three sailors, who found the spider legs to be fragile. One spider suffered a damaged and useless leg from one sailor; the second spider suffered two injured and useless legs by a second sailor; and the third spider suffered three damaged and useless legs from the third sailor's attack. The spiders quickly departed.

Which sailor was able to inflict damage to one spider leg, which to two legs, and which to three legs?

1. If the spider with six useful legs was not injured by Singood, then the spider with seven useful legs was injured by Singood.

2. The spider with seven useful legs was injured by the second mate only if the spider with five useful legs was injured by Singood.
3. The spider with six useful legs was not injured by the first mate only if the spider with five useful legs was injured by Singood.
4. The spider with seven legs was injured by Singood only if the spider with six useful legs was not injured by the first mate.

	7 legs	6 legs	5 legs
Singood			
1st mate			
2nd mate			

Solution on page 336

P1-10 Serpentmares!

Considering the terrifying adventures that Singood was experiencing, it is no wonder that he was having nightmares. One night he dreamed that four giant serpents—a red one, a black one, a yellow one, and a green one—attacked the three sailors and each was devoured by one of the serpents. No serpent devoured more than one sailor, and the red serpent definitely had a sailor meal.

In the nightmare, which sailor was devoured by which giant serpent?

1. If the second mate was not devoured by either the blue or green serpent, then the first mate was devoured by the red serpent.
2. The second mate was devoured by the blue serpent, unless the first mate was devoured by the red serpent.
3. If Singood was not devoured by either the black serpent or the blue serpent, then the second mate was devoured by the red serpent.
4. If Singood was devoured by the blue serpent, then the first mate was not devoured by the red serpent

	black	blue	green	red
Singood				
1st mate				
2nd mate				

Solution on page 337

P1-11 Contest on the Beach

When the three shipmates arrived back at the sea, their ship was nowhere to be seen. There was nothing to do but wait until their ship returned for them or another ship was sighted. During their long wait, to relieve their boredom they decided to have a contest, consisting of three events: a race down the beach, a coconut throw, and a tree climb. Each sailor won one of the three events.

From the statements below, who were the winners of the three events?

1. If the first mate won the race down the beach, then Singood won the coconut throw.
2. If the second mate won the coconut throw, then the first mate won the race.
3. If the second mate won the tree climb, then the first mate won the coconut throw.
4. If the second mate won the race down the beach, then Singood won the tree climb.
5. If Singood won the race down the beach, then the first mate won the tree climb.

	coconut	race	tree climb
Singood			
1st mate			
2nd mate			

Solution on page 338

P1-12 The Rescue

The sailors waited for rescue for what seemed a long time. Finally, one day, there appeared on the horizon not one but three ships. One ship had three masts and two had four masts. One ship was black, one was green, and one was white. Which one of the three ships rescued the sailors, and how many masts did it have?

1. If the three sailors were not rescued by the white ship, then the rescue ship had four masts.
2. The three sailors were rescued by a black ship, unless it did not have four masts.
3. If the rescue ship was black, then it did not have four masts.
4. If the rescue ship had four masts, then it was green.
5. If the rescue ship had three masts, then it was not white.

	black	green	white
color			
masts			

Mark a plus sign for color, and a 3 or 4 for masts.

Solution on page 339

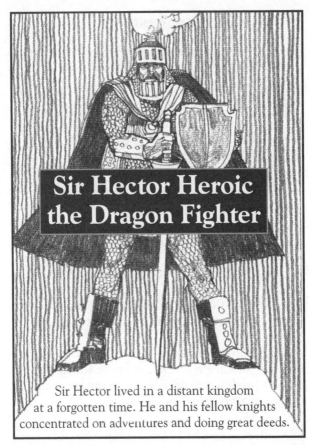

Sir Hector Heroic the Dragon Fighter

Sir Hector lived in a distant kingdom
at a forgotten time. He and his fellow knights
concentrated on adventures and doing great deeds.

P1-13 A Contest

The dragons in the land had begun to lose their fear and were becoming a serious threat to farm animals, and to vulnerable villagers. The king therefore proclaimed that a contest be held. In one period, sunrise to sunset, knights were to boldly confront as many dragons as they could and either slay them or frighten them so that the dragons would retreat to faraway places. The deemed winner of the contest was to receive a grand prize.

On the eve of the contest, two knights rode deep into the backcountry, where many of the marauding dragons lived, and camped there overnight in order to gain an advantage over other knights.

The winner proved to be either Sir Hector, Sir Able, Sir Bold, or Sir Gallant. From the statements below, who was the contest winner?

1. If Sir Able won the contest, then he concentrated on only the largest dragons in the land.
2. If Sir Hector won the contest, then he did not forget his shield.
3. If Sir Gallant won the contest, then he was the only knight who camped out overnight in the backcountry.
4. Sir Hector was an excellent cook, and during his night in the backcountry, he enjoyed a sumptuous dinner.
5. Sir Able had to quit when his captive mouse, which he kept to attract his prey, escaped.
6. If Sir Hector remembered his shield, then his squire forgot to pack his food.

	Sir Able	Sir Bold	Sir Gallant	Sir Hector
winner				

Indicate a plus or minus as you form your conclusions.

Solution on page 340

P1-14 Seeking Adventure

Craving some excitement, Sir Hector, Sir Able, Sir Bold, and Sir Gallant set out in search of adventure. During their travels, two battled dragons, one battled a giant, and one had a confrontation with a sorcerer.

From the statements below, which knight had which adventure?

1. If Sir Gallant did not confront a sorcerer, then Sir Hector battled a dragon.
2. If Sir Hector did not battle a giant, then Sir Able battled a giant.
3. Sir Bold confronted a sorcerer, if he did not battle a giant.

	dragons	giant	sorcerer
Sir Able			
Sir Bold			
Sir Gallant			
Sir Hector			

Solution on page 341

P1-15 The Sword-Fighting Matches

During one tournament, Sir Hector, Sir Able, and Sir Bold were each involved in a sword-fighting match. Two of the knights won their matches and one knight lost. Which two knights won and which knight lost?

1. Sir Able won his match, if Sir Hector lost his match.
2. If Sir Hector won his match, then Sir Bold lost his match.
3. Sir Able lost his match, if Sir Bold won his match.

	Sir Able	Sir Bold	Sir Hector
won			
lost			

Solution on page 341–342

P1-16 Murder in the Black Castle

It was a dark night, heavy with wind and rain, when three lone knights, strangers to each other, chanced to meet in front of a black and gloomy castle. They were suspicious of each other, but, as was their custom, they approached the castle and sought refuge for the night. The three knights were greeted by a sour-faced servant who explained that the master had retired for the evening but that their needs would be met. The three strangers were then provided food and shown to separate rooms.

Sometime during the night a murder was committed. The crime can be considered somewhat unusual, as not only is the culprit unknown but the identity of the victim is also unclear. Fortunately, the list of possible culprits and victims can be narrowed to five; the servant, the master, and the three knights.

Given the following clues, who was the victim and who was the culprit?

1. If the knight in room 1 was the culprit, the knight in room 3 was the victim.
2. If the knight in room 2 was the victim, the servant was the culprit.
3. If the knight in room 3 was the victim, the knight in room 2 was the culprit.
4. If the servant was the culprit, the victim was the knight in room 3.
5. The servant was not available until the next morning, and was not able to provide an alibi.
6. If the knight in room 3 was the culprit, the knight in room 2 was the victim.
7. If the knight in room 2 was the culprit, the servant was the victim.

	victim	culprit
room 1		
room 2		
room 3		
servant		
master		

Solution on pages 342–343

P1-17 The Mysterious Masked Miscreant

A mysterious masked miscreant was a thorn in Sir Hector's side. He was a villainous type, guilty of many wrong deeds. Sir Hector finally tracked him down, and the two faced each other, prepared for a fight to the finish. The time of day was morning, early afternoon, or early evening.

From the statements that follow, what was the outcome of the confrontation?

1. If Sir Hector pulled off the miscreant's mask and was overwhelmed by the evil face that he saw, then it was morning.
2. If Sir Hector's fellow knights arrived just in time to save him, then it was early afternoon.
3. If it was morning, then Sir Hector had forgotten his sword so didn't stay to do battle.
4. If it was early evening, then Sir Hector's fellow knights arrived just in time to save him.
5. If it was early afternoon, then Sir Hector pulled off the miscreant's mask and was overwhelmed by the evil face that he saw.

	over- whelmed	knights arrived	forgot sword
Sir Hector			
miscreant			

Solution on pages 343–344

P1-18 Who Saw Which Giant?

Most of the giants in the land were peaceful fellows who tended to keep to themselves. However, one lone giant, whose identity is in question, had been taking farm animals at night, causing distress among the farmers. Sir Hector, Sir Able, and Sir Bold offered their help in identifying the culprit, each having seen the thief. Their accounts, though, gave rise to two suspects, giant number one and giant number two.

When a crime has been committed, it's well-known that witnesses often have difficulty recalling what they have seen with any high degree of accuracy. Following are four statements drawn from descriptions of what the three knights claimed to have seen, and assumptions as to the accuracies or inaccuracies of their observations:

1. If giant number one was guilty, then Sir Hector's description was accurate.
2. If Sir Able's description was inaccurate, then giant number two was guilty.
3. If Sir Bold's description was accurate, then Sir Able's description was inaccurate.

4. If Sir Hector's description was accurate, then Sir Bold's description was accurate.

Which of the two giants was guilty?

	giant #1	giant #2
guilty		

Solution on page 344

P1-19 Sir Hector's Most Challenging Adventure

Sir Hector has had many exciting and challenging adventures. When asked which of his past adventures was the most challenging, the brave knight was only able to narrow the list to five. These included the encounter with Grimsby the Giant, the confrontation with the sorcerer, the confrontation with the mysterious masked miscreant, the confrontation with the ancient dragon, and the rescue from the black tower, not necessarily in that order.

From the following statements, can you determine which of Sir Hector's past adventures was the most challenging?

1. If neither the encounter with Grimsby the Giant nor the confrontation with the mysterious masked miscreant was the most challenging adventure, then the confrontation with the ancient dragon was the second most challenging.

2. If the confrontation with the ancient dragon was the second most challenging, then neither the rescue from the black tower nor

the confrontation with the sorcerer was the most challenging.

3. If neither the encounter with Grimsby the Giant nor the confrontation with the sorcerer was the second most challenging, then either the confrontation with the mysterious masked miscreant or the confrontation with the ancient dragon was the most challenging.

4. If the confrontation with the sorcerer was the second most challenging, then the rescue from the black tower was the most challenging.

most
challenging

dragon	
miscreant	
giant	
tower	
sorcerer	

Solution on page 345

P1-20 Four Fair Damsels in Distress

Sir Hector was famous throughout the land for his rescuing of fair damsels in distress. It was said that he had rescued four: Maid Marie, Maid Mary, Maid Morgana, and Maid Matilda. One was rescued from a castle tower where she had been kept by a sorcerer, one from a dragon's lair, one from two giants that were busy fighting over her, and one from the mysterious masked miscreant's hideout.

From the statements below, which fair damsel was rescued from which predicament?

1. If Maid Morgana was not rescued from the miscreant's hideout, then Maid Marie was rescued from a castle tower.
2. Maid Matilda was rescued from the miscreant's hideout, unless Maid Mary found her way home alone from the dragon's lair.
3. If Maid Marie was rescued from a castle tower, then Maid Mary was rescued from two giants.
4. If Maid Matilda was not rescued from the miscreant's hideout, then neither was Maid Morgana.

	2 giants	castle	dragon	miscreant
Maid Marie				
Maid Mary				
Maid Matilda				
Maid Morgana				

Solution on page 346

P1-21 Encounter with a Gigantic Serpentlike Creature

Farmers in the land had sorely complained about a strange, giant, serpentlike creature that was eating livestock, as well as pets and children. Sir Hector, Sir Gallant, and Sir Resolute were determined to confront this gigantic and ferocious beast.

When they encountered the creature, it appeared not nearly as large or ferocious as described. The three decided that one knight should be enough to dispose of this fearful menace. One of the knights went home, one fought the creature, and one stayed to observe. After a short skirmish, the creature agreed to leave for good. The heroic knights later returned to accept the farmers' adulations.

Which knight actually fought the creature, which one stayed to observe, and which one went home?

1. If Sir Gallant did the fighting, then Sir Hector observed.
2. If Sir Hector did the fighting, then Sir Gallant went home.

3. If Sir Gallant went home, then Sir Resolute observed.
4. If Sir Resolute observed, then Sir Gallant did the fighting.
5. If Sir Hector observed, then Sir Resolute did the fighting.

	fought	observed	went home
Sir Hector			
Sir Gallant			
Sir Resolute			

Solution on page 347

P1-22 Confrontation with the Giant

A giant was taking livestock and terrorizing the people of the land. Sir Hector and his fellow knights, Sir Able, Sir Bold, Sir Gallant, Sir Resolute, and Sir Victor, decided that two of them should confront this giant and drive him from the land. The two adventurers armed themselves and rode to do combat.

When they approached the giant, a short but fierce battle ensued. It was at this point that the giant happened to think of another land, one where he would not encounter so much resistance, and he quickly retreated, leaving for parts unknown. From the following statements, which two of the knights confronted the giant?

1. If neither Sir Hector nor Sir Victor confronted the giant, then Sir Gallant did.
2. If either Sir Gallant or Sir Victor confronted the giant, then Sir Able did not.
3. If neither Sir Able nor Sir Hector confronted the giant, then Sir Resolute did.
4. If neither Sir Bold nor Sir Able confronted the giant, then Sir Victor did.

5. If Sir Hector confronted the giant, then either Sir Gallant or Sir Resolute did.
6. If Sir Victor was not one of the two who confronted the giant, then neither was Sir Able nor Sir Resolute.

	Hector	Able	Bold	Gallant	Resolute	Victor
Hector						
Able						
Bold						
Gallant						
Resolute						
Victor						

Solution on pages 348–349

P1-23 Victory at the Grand Tournament

Sir Hector, Sir Able, Sir Bold, Sir Gallant, and Sir Resolute each entered the big annual tournament, which attracted knights from all over the land. Two of the five brave knights were victorious over the others, and, since neither would compete against his comrade, they shared the grand prize.

From the statements that follow, which two were victorious?

1. If Sir Gallant was victorious, then Sir Hector was not victorious.
2. If Sir Able was victorious, then Sir Gallant was not victorious.
3. If Sir Hector was not victorious, then Sir Bold was not victorious.
4. If Sir Resolute was victorious, then Sir Able was victorious.
5. If Sir Bold was victorious, then Sir Able was not victorious.
6. Sir Resolute was victorious, if Sir Hector was victorious.

	victorious
Sir Able	
Sir Bold	
Sir Gallant	
Sir Hector	
Sir Resolute	

Solution on pages 349–350

P1-24 Knights' Adversaries

Sir Hector, Sir Able, Sir Bold, and Sir Gallant were each especially skilled at dealing with a certain type of adversary. For one knight it was giant serpents, for one it was dragons, for one it was giants, and for one it was sorcerers.

Based on the following statements, determine which knight was most skilled at dealing with which type of adversary.

1. If Sir Able was the most skilled at dealing with dragons, then Sir Gallant was the most skilled at dealing with giants.
2. If Sir Bold was the most skilled at dealing with giants, then Sir Hector was the most skilled at dealing with sorcerers.
3. If Sir Bold was the most skilled at dealing with sorcerers, then Sir Able was the most skilled at dealing with dragons.
4. If Sir Gallant was not the most skilled at dealing with dragons, then Sir Hector was the most skilled at dealing with giants.
5. If Sir Gallant was the most skilled at dealing with giant serpents, then Sir Bold was not the most skilled at dealing with dragons.

6. If Sir Hector was the most skilled at dealing with sorcerers, then Sir Able was the most skilled at dealing with giants.

7. If Sir Able was the most skilled at dealing with giants, then Sir Gallant was the most skilled at dealing with sorcerers.

	dragons	giants	serpents	sorcerers
Sir Able				
Sir Bold				
Sir Gallant				
Sir Hector				

Solution on pages 350–351

2.
Who Dunnit?

The puzzles in this section involve crimes that have been committed. Your challenge in each puzzle is to determine who is guilty. In each case there are suspects who make statements. To solve each puzzle you must decide who is telling the truth and who is not.

P2-1 Supermarket Theft

A supermarket theft has occurred. Someone took a fully loaded cart without paying for the groceries. One of three suspects is guilty—but which one? The guilty party's statement is true; the other two are false.

Who is guilty?

A. B took the cart loaded with groceries.

B. A's statement is true.

C. A's statement is false.

```
A ┌──────────┐
  ├──────────┤
B ├──────────┤
  ├──────────┤
C └──────────┘
```

Indicate F (False) or T (True) in the boxes as you draw your conclusions.

Solution on page 352

P2-2 Bicycle Thefts

Several bicycles have been stolen in town. It is the work of one person and there are three suspects. Their statements are below. The statement by the guilty party is false; the other two statements are true.

Who is guilty?

A. C did it.

B. A's statement is false.

C. B's statement is true.

A	
B	
C	

Solution on page 353

P2-3 Pool Party Push

It was a fun party out by the pool until someone pushed Janie into the water, fully clothed. No one could be quite sure who did it, but the list of suspects was narrowed down to four. Here, they each make one statement. However, only one of the four suspects speaks truthfully. The guilty party can be deduced from their statements.

Who did it?

A. Either B or C did it.

B. I did it.

C. D did it.

D. A did it.

A
B
C
D

Solution on pages 353–354

P2-4 The Impostor Surgeon

An out-of-work medical technician posed as a veterinarian surgeon and successfully performed several operations on small animals before he was discovered. However, because he always was only seen wearing a surgical mask, his identity was in question.

There are three suspects, one of whom is the impostor. Each suspect makes two statements. The impostor makes one true and one false statement. The veracity of the other two suspects is unknown.

Which one is the impostor?

A. 1. C did it because he wanted to help animals.
   2. B's first statement is true.

B. 1. I am innocent.
   2. A is the impostor.

C. 1. A's second statement is true.
   2. B's second statement is false.

	1	2
A		
B		
C		

Solution on page 354

P2-5 Granny Smith's Famous Pecan Pie

Everyone simply raved about Granny Smith's pecan pie! It was famous throughout the county. One day, just before a big Sunday dinner, her famous creation disappeared from the back porch where it had been cooling, never to be seen again.

There were four suspects. Each made a statement, but only one spoke the truth. Their statements are below.

Who did it?

A. I did it.

B. Either A or I did it.

C. D did it.

D. B did it.

A

B

C

D

Solution on page 355

P2-6 Two Scam Hustlers

Two hustlers were working a scam together. They were attempting to convince elderly people that they could double their money if they would give them their Social Security checks.

Five suspects have been identified. Each one makes a statement. The two guilty ones make false statements. The other three make true statements.

Which two are guilty?

A. E is not one of the guilty parties.

B. C is not guilty.

C. D is innocent.

D. If B is not guilty, then A is guilty.

E. C is guilty.

A
B
C
D
E

Solution on pages 355–356

P2-7 Who Stole the Goat?

Two semi-pro football teams are arch rivals. One member of the Lions stole the mascot of the rival team, the Goats, the night before the big game and didn't return it until the day after the game. There are four suspects: the quarterback, the center, the running back, and the defensive end. Each makes two statements.

The statements by the quarterback and the center are false, the running back makes one true and one false statement, and the defensive end makes two true statements.

From their statements below, which one is which suspect, and who did it?

A. 1. I am not the running back.
   2. The center did it.

B. 1. I am not the quarterback.
   2. The running back did it.

C. 1. I am not the center.
   2. The defensive end did it.

D. 1. I am not the defensive end.
   2. The quarterback did it.

	1	2	football position
A			
B			
C			
D			

Solution on pages 356–357

P2-8 What's the Crime?

A crime has been committed. The police are not sure what it is, but there are three suspects and they all have disreputable reputations. They make the statements below. Each makes one true and two false statements. What was the crime and which suspect did it?

A. 1. I stole a car.
   2. B is innocent.
   3. C is a disreputable person.

B. 1. I robbed a service station.
   2. I stole a car.
   3. A is guilty.

C. 1. I robbed a service station.
   2. B's first statement is false.
   3. A is innocent.

	1	2	3
A			
B			
C			

Solution on page 357

P2-9 The Hood-Ornament Thefts

A thief was stealing Mercedes-Benz hood ornaments and selling them for use as necklaces. The sheriff interrogated four suspects who had been seen hanging around the Mercedes-Benz dealership. Their statements are below.

Little is known as to the suspects' truthfulness except that only one of the guilty party's statements is true.

A. 1. I wouldn't recognize a Mercedes Benz if I saw one.
   2. B didn't do it.

B. 1. A's second statement is true.
   2. A did it.

C. 1. A would certainly recognize a Mercedes Benz if he saw one.
   2. At least one of B's statements is true.

D. 1. Both of B's statements are false.
   2. I wouldn't recognize a Mercedes Benz if I saw one.

	1	2
A		
B		
C		
D		

Solution on page 358

P2-10 Thanksgiving Dinner

Mrs. Olsen had spent all day preparing for a festive Thanksgiving family dinner. The family was enjoying refreshments in the living room before dinner. The cooked turkey, which had been set near the kitchen door in readiness for the feast, disappeared—taken by a thief who had apparently smelled the mouthwatering turkey aroma through an open window.

Three suspects were identified and one of them is guilty. Their statements are below. Each suspect makes at least one false statement.

Who stole the turkey?

A. 1. Either B or I did it.
   2. I agree with B's second statement.

B. 1. I agree with A's first statement.
   2. C is innocent.

C. 1. I agree with A's second statement.
   2. A did it and B helped him.

	1	2
A		
B		
C		

Solution on page 358–359

P2-11 Car Thefts

In a southern Arizona town, several Ford Mustangs have been stolen, apparently to be sold in Mexico. Three suspects, known thieves, have been identified. One of them is guilty.

One suspect makes three true statements, and one makes three false statements. How the third suspect responds is unknown. Which one stole the Mustangs?

A. 1. I am innocent.
   2. All of my statements are untruthful.
   3. I am opposed to all crime, especially car thefts.

B. 1. I did not do it.
   2. Only one of my statements is untruthful.
   3. I am opposed to all crime, especially car thefts.

C. 1. I did not do it.
   2. I always speak truthfully.
   3. I understand that Ford Mustangs are popular in Mexico.

	1	2	3
A			
B			
C			

Solution on page 359

P2-12 Residence Burglaries

A series of residence burglaries has caused concern in the neighborhood. The police inspector concentrated on solving these crimes and has come up with three suspects. One of them is guilty.

The suspects make the following statements. Each suspect makes at least two false statements.

Who is the burglar?

A. 1. B and C are strangers to each other.
   2. I am the burglar.
   3. B's second statement is not truthful.

B. 1. I don't know C.
   2. C is the burglar.
   3. A's third statement is false.

C. 1. A is the burglar.
   2. I am acquainted with B.
   3. If I had wanted to be a burglar, I would have picked a more affluent neighborhood.

	1	2	3
A			
B			
C			

Solution on page 360

P2-13 Who Murdered Quick-Hands Eddie?

Quick-Hands Eddie has been, as they say, "offed." The police have identified three witnesses. They each claim to know who did it. However, they don't seem to be able to agree as to the identity of the guilty party, as each claims a different culprit, all three of whom are known criminals with a tendency toward violent crimes.

Each witness makes three statements below. However, two of the witnesses make no true statements. The truthfulness of the third witness is unknown.

Who did it?

A. 1. I saw Rocky do it.
    2. Harry did not do it.
    3. Phil would not hurt a fly.

B. 1. A's second statement is false.
    2. Harry the Hulk did it.
    3. Like me, Rocky is an upstanding citizen.

C.   1.   Phil the Enforcer is the culprit.
      2.   B's statements are all true.
      3.   I agree with A's second statement.

	1	2	3
A			
B			
C			

Solution on page 361

P2-14 Who Cheated at Poker?

Five poker players were enjoying a game when, during one hand, five aces turned up. Clearly, someone had cheated.

The players' statements follow. Each makes one true and one false statement. Who cheated?

A. 1. I am certainly innocent.
    2. I have no idea who cheated.

B. 1. C is innocent.
    2. Neither A nor D cheated.

C. 1. B's first statement is true.
    2. B was the cheater.

D. 1. B did it.
    2. B's second statement is true.

E. 1. A was one of the players that day.
    2. D's second statement is false.

	1	2
A		
B		
C		
D		
E		

Solution on page 362

P2-15 Which of the Three Is Innocent?

Two crimes have been committed in the Williamson family. The culprits are two of the family's three boys. However, all three confess. Perhaps the third boy did not want to be different.

At any rate, the two culprits truthfully admit their crimes and the third boy falsely confesses to a crime. Each boy makes one true and two false statements.

Which boy is innocent?

Junior
1. Timmy's first statement is false.
2. Sonny's first statement is true.
3. I took some money from the dresser.

Sonny
1. I played hooky from school today.
2. Timmy's first statement is false.
3. Junior's third statement is false.

Timmy
1. I kicked the dog.
2. Sonny's first statement is true.
3. Junior's third statement is false.

	1	2	3
Junior			
Sonny			
Timmy			

Solution on pages 362–363

P2-16 Who Put the Rattlesnake in Henry's Garage?

"I suppose it was just a prank," Henry said. The fact, though, is that rattlesnakes are quite dangerous and somebody did put a live one in Henry's garage.

There are three suspects. Their statements are true except for any directly mentioning the culprit. Which one is guilty?

A. 1. C is not guilty.
   2. Rattlesnakes are not good for you.

B. 1. A's first statement is false.
   2. C's first statement is true.

C. 1. I wouldn't go near a rattlesnake.
   2. A is not guilty.

	1	2
A		
B		
C		

Solution on pages 363–364

P2-17 Theft of a Suit from Fred's Men's Fashions

A thief tried on a suit in Fred's clothing store while Fred wasn't looking and then calmly walked out of the store without paying. There are four suspects, all of whom were seen trying on suits. Their statements are below.

One suspect makes three true statements; one makes two true and one false statement; one makes one true and two false statements; and one makes three false statements. Which one is the thief?

A. 1. D didn't do it.
   2. Neither B nor I stole that suit.
   3. I would never wear a suit.

B. 1. Only one of the four of us is guilty.
   2. C did it.
   3. D already had a suit.

C. 1. A would wear a suit.
   2. Neither D nor I did it.
   3. My suit is worn out.

D. 1. A did it.
   2. B is innocent.
   3. I didn't have a suit.

	1	2	3
A			
B			
C			
D			

Solution on pages 364–365

P2-18 Stolen Golf Clubs

At the Mountain Golf Club, a set of expensive left-handed golf clubs has been stolen. The evidence points to three of the club's employees who were on duty during the time that the golf clubs were taken and who are known to be left-handed golfers. One of these employees did it.

Each makes three statements, although no two suspects make the same number of true statements. Which suspect is guilty?

A. 1. C is left-handed.
    2. B's statements are all false.
    3. I don't play golf.

B. 1. A's first statement is true.
    2. C' first statement is true.
    3. A took the golf clubs.

C. 1. B is not guilty.
    2. B was on duty during the time of the theft.
    3. I am not left-handed.

	1	2	3
A			
B			
C			

Solution on pages 365–366

P2-19 Who Stole the Baseball Mitt?

A famous baseball player was in the city to play in a game. Just before it was to begin, the discovery was made that the player's favorite mitt had been stolen. The police were able to identify and question three suspects who had been seen hanging around the club-house and were known to sell stolen property. One of them stole the mitt.

Each suspect makes the same number of true and false statements. Which one is the thief?

A. 1. I have a record of committing this type of crime.
   2. C did it.
   3. B does not need it, so he would not have stolen it.

B. 1. I don't need it, so I would not have stolen it.
   2. I'm sure neither C nor I would commit a crime.
   3. A has a record of committing this type of crime.

C. 1. A is not a likely suspect.
   2. B did it.
   3. B's first statement is false.

	1	2	3
A			
B			
C			

Solution on pages 366–367

P2-20 Who Stole Golf Cart No. 22?

One Halloween night, four revelers were having a great time being mischievous in the vicinity of the Mountain Golf Club, when their fun got out of hand. One of the four, in the presence of the other three, stole a golf cart and proceeded to drive it over several greens, damaging them.

The next day, the four revelers were questioned, and only one of them made no false statements.

Which one stole the cart and damaged the greens?

A. 1. I wasn't there.
   2. B was looking for trouble; she did it.
   3. When I arrived, the damage was done.

B. 1. I was there.
   2. C stole the cart.
   3. A is innocent; he tried to stop it.

C. 1. A's first statement is true.
   2. D did it.
   3. A's third statement is false.

D. 1. C's third statement is false.
   2. A's first statement is false.
   3. Neither B nor I did it.

	1	2	3
A			
B			
C			
D			

Solution on page 367

P2-21 Unsavory Characters

A load of Christmas toys that had just arrived at the local toy store was stolen. Four individuals who had unsavory reputations were questioned by the police. Each had been seen in the area and all four know who stole the toys.

The guilty party makes one true and two false statements. The truthfulness of the statements by the other suspects is unknown.

A. 1. I was out of town when the theft occurred.
   2. D is guilty.
   3. I think the toys were just lost.

B. 1. A lied when he said he was out of town.
   2. C is innocent.
   3. I do not understand why I am a suspect.

C. 1. A lied when he said he was out of
town when the theft occurred.
2. I am innocent.
3. I'll bet A knows who did it.

D. 1. I understand why I am suspect.
2. C is guilty.
3. I am innocent.

	1	2	3
A			
B			
C			
D			

Solution on page 368

P2-22 Who Is the Shoplifter?

There has been a series of shoplifting thefts from stores in the town mall. Thanks to careful observations on the part of employees in several stores, three suspects have been identified, and it is clear that one of them is guilty.

Their statements follow. However, the culprit makes three false statements; one of the other two suspects makes two true statements and one false statement; and one makes one true and two false statements.

Which one is the shoplifter?

A. 1. C's first statement is false.
   2. C did it.
   3. I am not the most likely suspect.

B. 1. A is the most likely suspect.
   2. I only heard about the thefts later.
   3. I am innocent.

C. 1. B's first statement is not true.
   2. A did it.
   3. B's second statement is false.

	1	2	3
A			
B			
C			

Solution on page 369

P2-23 Who Stole the Prime Steaks?

The owner of Morgan's Meats had a large commercial refrigerator full of prime steaks for sale. One night, a thief gained entrance to the refrigerator and stole the entire load of expensive steaks, enough to require a truck to transport them.

Three suspects were questioned. Each is a known thief who is capable of finding a buyer for the whole load of steaks. Their statements follow.

Each suspect makes two true and two false statements. Which one is guilty?

A. 1. Any day is a good day for a heist.
    2. I would have no buyer for that much loot.
    3. I took it on my motorcycle.
    4. I saw C take it.

B. 1. I don't have access to a truck.
    2. My statements are not all true.
    3. I am innocent.
    4. A's statements are all true.

C. 1. My statements are all false.
   2. B has access to a truck.
   3. We are all innocent.
   4. A has a buyer for the loot.

	1	2	3	4
A				
B				
C				

Solution on page 370

P2-24 Jewelry Theft

A very expensive and famous diamond necklace has been stolen from the local museum. Evidence indicates that the theft was planned and executed by a single individual. There are four suspects who were seen at the museum. All are known to be jewel thieves, and any one of them would have taken the necklace, if he or she had seen it. One of the four is the thief.

Their statements are below, although no two of them make the same number of false statements.

Which suspect is guilty?

A. 1. B is the culprit.
    2. I would have taken it, but it was gone when I got there.
    3. D and I planned to take it together.

B. 1. D did not take it.
    2. I would have taken it, but it was gone when I got there.
    3. D and I planned to take it together.

C. 1. B did not take it.
   2. A would have taken it, but it was gone when he got there.
   3. D and I planned to take it together.

D. 1. A is the thief.
   2. I did not plan with anyone to take it.
   3. B would have taken it, but it was gone when he got there.

	1	2	3
A			
B			
C			
D			

Solution on pages 371–372

P2-25 Who Aced Jake the Snake?

Jake the Snake has been murdered. He probably deserved his fate, as he was a thoroughly disreputable character. The list of people who were happy to hear that he was at last out of their lives is long indeed.

The number of actual suspects, though, has been narrowed to four who are themselves somewhat disreputable. One of them is guilty. Each makes two statements. In total, three statements are true and five statements are false.

Which one aced Jake the Snake?

A. 1. I did not do it.
   2. I am surprised and offended that I am a suspect.

B. 1. D did it.
   2. C's second statement is false.

C. 1. I am innocent.
   2. B is guilty.

D. 1. I did not do it.
   2. C must have done it.

	1	2
A		
B		
C		
D		

Solution on pages 372–373

P2-26 A Dead-Serious Poker Game

Upstairs in a private room over Johnny's Seven Seas Restaurant six players were engaged in a high-stakes poker game. Suddenly, after Joe had won a big hand, two of the other players accused the winner of cheating and both throttled him in front of the other three players.

Everyone, except of course Joe, makes statements to the local police, who had been called. Their truthfulness is unknown except that one of the guilty players makes two true statements and the other makes two false statements.

Which two players committed the crime?

A. 1. I was not involved in the game.
   2. D's first statement is false.

B. 1. E's statements are both false.
   2. I was not involved in the crime,
      and I do not know who was.

C. 1. A was not involved in the game.
   2. I stepped out of the room before the crime.

D. 1. The guilty players are A and C.
   2. E's statements are both true.

E. 1. C is not guilty.
   2. B's second statement is false.

	1	2
A		
B		
C		
D		
E		

Solution on pages 373–374

P2-27 Who Released the Desert Zoo Animals?

A small zoo contains animals native to the area. Four individuals decided that it would be fun to release several of the animals. Each one released a different animal. The animals were a bobcat, a javelina, a mountain lion, and a coyote. Two additional animals, a mountain goat and a gila monster, were also released. The six animals lost no time disappearing into the mountains.

The four culprits were apprehended and admitted their guilt, but there was some confusion as to who released which animal. Their statements are below.

The one who released the bobcat makes two true statements and one false statement; the one who released the coyote makes one true and two false statements; and the one who released the javelina and the one who released the mountain lion each make three false statements.

A. 1. I did not release the coyote.
   2. I did not release the mountain goat.
   3. D's first statement is false.

B. 1. I did not release the javelina.
   2. C did not release the coyote.
   3. I released the gila monster.

C. 1. I did not release the bobcat.
   2. I released two animals.
   3. A's first statement is false.

D. 1. I did not release the mountain lion.
   2. I released the gila monster.
   3. I agree with B's third statement.

	statements			animal released
	1	2	3	
A				
B				
C				
D				

Solution on pages 374–376

3.
Fragments

These puzzles offer statements that provide limited amounts of pertinent information. Just enough information is available in each puzzle to enable you to find the solution. The puzzles are divided into three types, as follows:

A's: The statements within the puzzles in this part are all true and contribute information to help you solve each puzzle.

B's: Each puzzle in this part includes a false statement. To arrive at the correct solution, you will need to determine which statement is false, and discard it.

C's: The statements within each puzzle in this part are all false except one. It will be necessary to identify the true statement in order to solve the puzzle.

The A's

The statements given in these puzzles are all true—no lies, no tricks. The information will guide you logically to the solutions.

P3-1a Four Vehicles

The Terrill family includes Mr. and Mrs. Terrill and their teenage son, Johnny. The family owns four vehicles: a roadster, a sedan, a popular new sports-utility vehicle, and a pickup truck. What vehicle is the usual transportation for each family member, and what is the color of each of the four vehicles?

1. Mr. Terrill drives the white vehicle, which is not the sedan, to and from work daily.
2. The truck has fewer miles on it than the yellow vehicle, the green vehicle, or the white vehicle.
3. The vehicle Johnny drives to school is not the roadster.
4. One vehicle, which is green, is over 50 years old and is used only during antique car rallies.
5. Mrs. Terrill prefers to drive the red vehicle.

	color	vehicle
Mr. Terrill		
Mrs. Terrill		
Johnny		
extra car		

Solution on pages 376–377

P3-2a Halloween Costumes

For Halloween one year four children, who are good friends, decided that they would each wear a different costume for trick-or-treating together. One wore a skeleton costume, one dressed up as a pirate, one wore a scary witch costume, and one dressed up as Robin Hood.

From the statements that follow, what is the surname (one is Finley) of each child, and what was the costume each wore?

1. Jimmy and Molly, neither of whom wore a pirate costume or a witch costume, are brother and sister.
2. The Smith boy lives across the street from Jimmy and Molly, he didn't wear a witch costume.
3. Billy lives several blocks away, and he didn't wear a pirate costume.
4. The one who wore a skeleton costume was the hit of the evening. He was not Sam.
5. One of the Dixons wore a Robin Hood costume.

	surname	costume
Billy		
Jimmy		
Molly		
Sam		

Solution on page 377

P3-3a Golfing Couples

Two married couples played a round of golf together. No two golfers had the same score, although the combined score of Mr. and Mrs. Albert was 187, the same as that of Mr. and Mrs. Baker.

From the statements below, determine the first name (one is Harry), surname, and score of each of the four players.

1. George didn't have the lowest score of the four players, but it was lower than the average score.
2. Kathryn's score was three strokes higher than Carol's.
3. There was only one stroke difference between the scores of Mr. and Mrs. Albert.
4. The average score of the two men was two strokes higher than the average score of the two women.

	surname	score
Carol		
George		
Harry		
Kathryn		

Solution on page 378

P3-4a Vacation Trips

Three couples from Santa Fe, New Mexico, planned vacation trips, each couple to a different location. The three destinations were Atlanta, GA, Tucson, AZ, and Santa Barbara, CA.

From the following statements, determine the first names (one is James and one is Jean) of the individuals and the surnames (one is Anderson) of each couple, and their destination.

1. Joyce said that they were going east to visit relatives.
2. Jack and his wife planned a golfing trip to Tucson.
3. John, his wife, and the Abernathys discussed their trips west while playing bridge together.
4. The Adamses don't play bridge.
5. Joan is not an Abernathy.

	surname	destination
Jack		
James		
Jean		
Joan		
John		
Joyce		

Solution on pages 378–379

P3-5a Accomplished Sisters

Four sisters, daughters of a Canadian diplomat, are musicians and also fluent in four European languages. Each plays a different musical instrument (the four instruments are the clarinet, the flute, the piano, and the violin) and each speaks a different language.

From the statements below, which sister plays which instrument and speaks which language (one is Italian)?

1. The sister who plays the clarinet does not speak French or German.
2. The sister who speaks Spanish especially likes her musical instrument, as she doesn't have to carry it to her music lessons.
3. Sheri doesn't speak German or Spanish, nor does she play the clarinet.
4. Ellen is not the girl who speaks German.
5. Neither Theresa, who doesn't play the flute, nor Ellen plays the clarinet.

	instrument	language
Ellen		
Renee		
Sheri		
Theresa		

Solution on page 379–380

P3-6a Summer Fun

One summer day, four children were engaged in some outdoor fun. Two were five years old. Of the other two, one was six and the other was seven.

From the statements that follow, determine the age of each child and the outdoor activity in which each was engaged. One was flying a kite, one was playing with a dog, and two were playing catch.

1. Neither Ted nor the one who was flying a kite is the oldest.
2. Neither of the two youngest was flying a kite.
3. Theresa is older than the boy with whom she was playing catch.
4. Neither Tony nor the child who is six was playing with a dog.
5. Timmy, who is not the oldest, was not playing catch; nor was Ted, who is not older than Timmy.

	age	activity
Ted		
Theresa		
Timmy		
Tony		

Solution on page 380

P3-7a Resort Activities

Three couples—the Taylors, the Thompsons, and the Tysons—spent their vacations together at a resort. Their first names, in some order, are Gene, Jean, Jerry, Geri, Pat, and Pat. Each couple concentrated on their favorite resort activity. For one couple it was golf; for a second couple it was tennis; and for the third couple it was horseback riding.

From the statements below, what is the first name of each husband and wife pair, and what was their surname and activity? No couple has first names that are phonetically the same.

1. Pat is a very good tennis player and she concentrated on this sport.
2. The Taylors and the Tysons played bridge each evening.
3. Taylor, who is not Pat, was saddle-sore after the first day at the resort.
4. Gene was so tired after each day's activity that he was content just to relax in the evening.
5. Pat became frustrated with all the delays on the golf course.

	surname	activity
Gene		
Geri		
Jean		
Jerry		
Pat		
Pat		

Solution on page 381

P3-8a Favorite Jazz Tunes

Five members of a jazz band play at the place called Johnny's Seven Seas Restaurant. When asked what their favorite jazz tunes were, each musician selected a different one.

From the following statements, what is the favorite tune selected by each of the musicians (one is *Lullaby of Birdland*)?

1. Mel's least favorites of the five tunes chosen are *Indiana* and *How High the Moon*."
2. Neither *Crazy Rhythm* nor *Sunny Side of the Street* is the favorite of Ansel.
3. Steve's favorite is one of Mel's least favorite of the five tunes chosen; the other one is Roger's favorite.
4. Caroline's favorite is not *Sunny Side of the Street*.
5. Steve doesn't understand why Roger doesn't like *Indiana*.

favorite tune

Ansel	
Caroline	
Mel	
Roger	
Steve	

Solution on pages 381–382

P3-9a Shopping at Martin's Men's Clothing

One day four friends shopped in Martin's clothing store at different times of the day, and each bought a different article of clothing.

From the statements that follow, what was each friend's full name (one surname was Thompson), what article did each buy, and in what order did they make their purchases?

1. Irwin, who did not buy the sweater, always shops early in the day.
2. Matthews, who shopped late that afternoon, was not the last of the four in the store.
3. Harry arrived at the store just before closing, and he was happy to find a sport coat that he liked.
4. Goodwin, who did not purchase the socks, shopped at lunchtime.
5. Hill, who bought a dress shirt, was the first to shop that day.
6. Frank shopped before George that day.

	surname	article	order of purchase
Frank			
George			
Harry			
Irwin			

Solution on pages 382–383

P3-10a Extreme Activities

Four couples, who are good friends, are addicted to extreme recreational activities, but each couple favors a different activity. From the following statements, what are the first names, surnames, and activity favored by each couple?

1. Otto received a broken arm two years ago from engaging in his favorite activity, which is not rock climbing.
2. Nate and his wife, who are not surnamed King, enjoy their favorite activity every chance they get.
3. Mike and his wife, the Kings, and the Ladues have been involved in their favorite activities for several years without an injury among them.
4. Ursula, who is not an Irvin or King, and Vicky and Sally like to debate their favorite activities: parachute jumping, rock climbing, and white-water rafting, in some order.
5. Neither the Jacksons nor the Irvins favor hang gliding nor white-water rafting.

6. Pete and his wife and Theresa and her husband enjoy an occasional dinner together.
7. Vicky holds a record number of parachute jumps by a woman.

	surname	activity
Mike		
Nate		
Otto		
Pete		
Sally		
Theresa		
Ursala		
Vicky		

Solution on pages 383–384

P3-11a College Reunion

Four former college football players attended a college reunion at their alma mater and enjoyed recalling old football experiences. Each now has a different occupation. From the following statements, what is each man's name, former position on the college football team, and current occupation?

1. Neither Jerry nor Mason was a defensive end or a center.
2. Joe and Jamie are the only ones who live in the same town as their former college; Morrison lives in another state.
3. Mayer, who isn't Joe, is a computer programmer.
4. The one who is the dentist was a quarterback; the one who was a linebacker is a financial consultant.
5. Mahoney and Jim both had to travel a significant distance to attend the reunion.
6. The lawyer (who was not a center), Jerry, and the financial consultant were close friends in college.

	surname	football position	occupation
Jamie			
Jerry			
Jim			
Joe			

Solution on page 385

P3-12a Dancing Couples

The local dance club features dances on weekend nights. Four married couples are among the active members, and each couple favors a different type of dance: one couple prefers waltzes, one favors the cha-cha, one prefers the rumba, and one prefers swing.

From the statements that follow, what is the first name of each husband (one is Sam) and wife (one is Gloria), what is the married name of each couple, and what type of dance does each couple prefer?

1. Stan and Walt, neither of whom is Campbell, sit down whenever swing music is played.
2. None of the Latin dances have any appeal for the Coles or the Conways.
3. Shirley and Betty agree that the waltz is not as much fun as other dances, but it's Anne's favorite.
4. Tom and Walt and their wives have been dance club members for many years.

5. The Conways and the Coles are relatively new members.
6. Betty and her husband moved from the other end of the country a year ago.
7. The Coles don't particularly care for waltzes.
8. Shirley, who isn't Carlson, considers the rumba to be her second-favorite dance.

	surname	dance
Anne		
Betty		
Gloria		
Sam		
Shirley		
Stan		
Tom		
Walt		

Solution on pages 386–387

P3-13a Favorite Outdoor Recreation

Five married couples enjoy outdoor recreation, although each couple favors a different sport. From the statements below, what is the full name (one given name is Harriet, one surname is Markham) of each husband and wife, and the favorite outdoor recreation of each couple?

1. Ginger and her husband, who is not Conrad or Doug, do not play golf or enjoy hiking.
2. The Nadlers, the Owenses, and Joyce and her husband are neighbors. Bob and his wife and the Kelsos live in different areas.
3. Fran and her husband, who is not Ed or Bob, spend as much time sailing as they can.
4. Al and his wife, who is not Irma or Ginger, like to tie their own trout flies.
5. The Lanes are excellent tennis players, and both like to enter tournaments.
6. Joyce and her husband, who is not Doug, would spend every day on the golf course if they could.

7. Al and his wife sometimes play bridge with their neighbors, the Owenses.
8. Conrad and his wife live a distance from the others, near the mountains where they can enjoy hiking.

	surname	recreation
Al		
Bob		
Conrad		
Doug		
Ed		
Fran		
Ginger		
Harriet		
Irma		
Joyce		

Solution on pages 387–388

P3-14a Neighbors' Houses

Five neighbors, the Quigleys, the Rodneys, the Smiths, the Taylors, and the Ungers, live either adjacent to or directly across the street from each other. Two of their houses are white, one is gray, one is green, and one is blue.

On which side of the street is each neighbor's house, and what is its color?

1. The two white houses are directly across the street from each other, at the west end of the street.
2. The Quigleys' house is not adjacent to either of the white houses.
3. The Rodneys' house is on the same side of the street as the Quigleys' house.
4. The blue house is immediately to the east of the Rodneys' house on the same side of the street.
5. The Smiths' house, which is not gray or white, is next door to the Ungers' house, which is on the south side of the street.
6. The Taylors' house is directly across the street from the Smiths' house.

	north side	south side	color
Quigley			
Rodney			
Smith			
Taylor			
Unger			

Solution on pages 388–389

P3-15a Tennis Tournament

Skyview Country Club is hosting its annual tennis tournament with Mountainside Country Club. Among those entered are three men and three women who are neighbors. Three are members of Skyview Country Club and three are members of Mountainside Country Club. One of the players is entered in the men's singles, one in the women's singles, one in the men's doubles, one in the women' doubles, and two in the mixed doubles.

What are the full names (one first name is Ruth) of each of the six players, in what event is each entered, and to which country club does each belong?

1. Of the Mountainside Country Club members, two are women.
2. Ms. Dixon, who is not Claire, and Ms. Gardner are playing in doubles events for different clubs.
3. Donald is one of his club's best players.
4. Jack Ernst and Phil, who is not Farrell, are both playing in doubles events for their club.

5. Anne Irwin is looking to defend her win from last year's competition.
6. Claire is counting on Hartland in their doubles match due to his experience.

	surname	event	country club
Anne			
Claire			
Donald			
Jack			
Phil			
Ruth			

Solution on pages 389–390

P3-16a Bridge Players

At a family reunion, four married couples played bridge at two tables. From the statements that follow, determine how the eight players were partnered and which ones were at which tables.

1. Mrs. Johnson partnered with her son-in-law.
2. Mr. Jones's partner was his wife's brother-in-law.
3. Mrs. Jones played against her sister.
4. Mr. Johnson played against his father-in-law.
5. Mrs. Smith's partner was her daughter.
6. Mrs. Williams partnered with her grandfather.
7. Mr. Johnson's partner was a man.

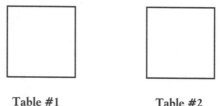

Table #1   Table #2

Solution on pages 390–391

P3-17a African Safari

Two couples who travel together frequently went on an African safari. In Botswana, the four were joined by two other couples who they were not previously acquainted with but were included in the safari.

The eight members of the group decided that it would be fun to see who would be the first to spot a different type of animal. They enjoyed catching sight of many animals during their time on safari. After each of the eight persons was the first to see a different type of animal, however, they lost interest in that game.

From the dozen statements given below, determine the full names (one surname is Mueller) of each safari member, and the type of animal first sighted by each of them.

1. Vern Dewitt was next to last to be the first to sight a different animal.
2. Eve, Lois, and Tina had not met before going on this safari trip.
3. Eve's spotting of a lion was the first sighting by the safari members.
4. Mrs. Duffy was the last to sight her different animal.

5. Mrs. Lundstrom was the first to see a giraffe.
6. A leopard was first sighted by Dan, whose wife was the first to sight a wildebeest.
7. Lundstrom and Dan were in a regular golf foursome back home.
8. A hyena was sighted just before a wildebeest was seen.
9. A cheetah was not sighted first by Tom, Mark, or either of the Duffys.
10. Margo's husband, Mark, was the first to sight a zebra.
11. Lois sighted her animal before Tina did.
12. Tom's wife, who is not Eve, was second to see an elephant.

	surname	animal first seen
Dan		
Eve		
Lois		
Margo		
Mark		
Tina		
Tom		
Vern		

Solution on pages 392–393

P3-18a The Father-and-Son Campout

Cub Scout Pack #28 recently held its annual father-and-son overnight campout. Five boys and their fathers attended. Based on the following statements, can you identify each boy's full name (one first name is Rickie, one surname is Albertson), age, and father's first name (one is David)?

The boys' ages are 9, 9½, 10 (two are 10), and 11 years old.

1. Jeff's son, who is not Eddie, is not one of the two ten-year-olds.
2. The oldest boy, who is not Jeff's son, lives across town from the Graysons, whose son is one of the ten-year-olds.
3. Mr. Dudley, whose son is one of the ten-year-olds, Bill, George, and Mr. Jackson, who is not Chuck's father, were in charge of putting up the tents.
4. The sons of James, Jeff, and Mr. Jackson are 11, 10, and 9, but not necessarily in that order.
5. Chuck and Eddie are the two oldest boys; Ned and Gary are the two youngest.

6. Gary and his father, Mr. Bradley and his son, and Bill and his son shared the cooking on the campout.
7. Mr. Grayson, whose son is not Chuck, Mr. Bradley, and George work for the same company.

boys' 1st names

	Chuck	Eddie	Gary	Ned	Rickie
Albertson					
Bradley					
Dudley					
Grayson					
Jackson					
Bill					
David					
George					
James					
Jeff					
ages					

boys' surnames (rows Albertson–Jackson)
fathers' 1st names (rows Bill–ages)

Solution on pages 393–394

P3-19a Knowheyan Physical Characteristics

The planet Knowhey is far beyond the known solar system. The Knowheyans are not unlike the inhabitants of Earth in many ways. There are, however, several differences. One peculiarity of the inhabitants of Knowhey is that they always speak using negative sentences. Several visitors to Knowhey are being accompanied by a Knowheyan interpreter, who is attempting to be helpful to them by describing the varied physical characteristics of the inhabitants.

From the interpreter's comments listed here regarding five Knowheyans, can you determine the height,

	3 m.	325 m.	3.5 m.	3.75 m.	4 m.
A					
B					
C					
D					
E					

age, and hair color of each? (Ages are 200, 220, 240, 260, and 280 Knowheyan years.)

1. The one who is 3.25 meters tall is not as old as the one who is 3 meters tall or as tall as the one with orange hair.
2. D, who is not 280 years old, does not have red hair.
3. A, who is not as old as D or the one with black hair, is not as young as C.
4. The one with silver hair is not as old as the one who has black hair or the one who is 3.5 meters tall, who is not as young as the one who has red hair.

NOTE: Additional statements and chart on following page.

200	220	240	260	280

5. The one who is 3.75 meters tall is not as old as the one who has silver hair, who is not as young as the one who is 4 meters tall.
6. C is not as old as E, who is not as old as the one who is 3.5 meters tall.
7. The one who has golden hair is not older or shorter than the one who has black hair.
8. E is not as short as the one who has golden hair or the one who is 240 years old, or as tall as the one who has orange hair.

	black	golden	orange	red	silver
A					
B					
C					
D					
E					

Solution on pages 395–396

P3-20a Fishing Tournament

The Clear Lake Anglers Club sponsored a bass fishing tournament. Five anglers competed, and each was accompanied on the lake by one of the official observers, who measured, weighed, and released each fish caught. Points were earned in four categories, as follows:

> Greatest total weight of fish caught: 4 points
> Most fish caught: 3 points
> Largest fish caught: 2 points
> Second-largest fish caught: 1 point
> Winning more than one category: 1 bonus point

Three of the five contestants won the four categories, and first place in the tournament was a tie between two anglers who finished with the same number of points. No two used the same type of casting lure.

From the statements listed on the next page, what is the first name (one is Kevin) and surname of each contestant; what casting lure did each use (one of the lures was a wounded-minnow bait); who won which categories; and which two shared the first-place prize?

1. Mike, who was one of the category winners, Black, who is not Terry, and the one who used the plastic worm live near each other.
2. Vick, who did not win the total weight category, did not use a spinner bait; nor did McNess.
3. The one who used a weighted jig, who was not Terry, did not win any of the categories.
4. Neither Sam nor Larson live near any of the other three contestants, nor did either use a spinner bait or a deep-running crank bait.
5. The angler who won the largest-fish category, who was not Smith, used a spinner bait.
6. Jones, who caught the most fish, did not use a deep-running crank bait.
7. Both McNess, who did not use a deep-running crank bait, and Terry, who did not use a plastic worm, had boat trouble and got started after the others.

Solution on pages 397–399

	Black	Jones	Larson	McNess	Smith
Kevin					
Mike					
Sam					
Terry					
Vick					
total weight					
most fish					
largest fish					
2nd-lgst. fish					
bonus					
crank bait					
plastic worm					
spinner bait					
weighted jig					
minnow bait					

The B's

In this next section, the puzzles each contain a series of statements. However, in each of these puzzles you will find that one statement is false. It will be necessary for you to identify the false one in order to solve the puzzle.

P3-21b Lost in Rome and Paris

Four ladies decided on a vacation in Europe. They made plans to visit many of the historic sights in Rome and Paris. They began their vacation in Rome, and when they arrived, they started to take in the beauties of this famous city. The four sights they most looked forward to in Rome were the Colosseum, the Sistine Chapel, St. Peter's Basilica, and the Trevi Fountain.

Somehow, in the crowd they became separated from one another and, unable to speak the language, each became hopelessly lost. Independently, each eventually came upon one of the sights that they had longed to see, found their bearings, and were able to get back together and complete the rest of their stay in Rome, as planned.

The next stop in their tour was Paris. There, the four sights that they planned to visit were the Eiffel Tower, the Louvre Museum, the Moulin Rouge, and Notre Dame Cathedral. On arriving in Paris, they again became separated from each other in the crowd. Once again, each independently happened upon one of the sights they had looked forward to seeing. After regrouping, they finally managed to stay together and enjoy the rest of their trip without further mishap.

From the statements that follow, one of which is false, what famous sights—one in Rome and one in Paris—did each traveler inadvertently come upon?

1. Eleanor did not come upon the Sistine Chapel, the Trevi Fountain, or St. Peter's Basilica.
2. Frances came upon either the Eiffel Tower or the Moulin Rouge Cabaret.
3. The one who came upon the Colosseum came upon the Eiffel Tower.
4. Between Frances and Eleanor, one of them came upon the Notre Dame Cathedral and the other came upon the Eiffel Tower.
5. Betty came upon either the Sistine Chapel or the Colosseum.
6. Either Frances or Betty came upon the Colosseum.
7. Betty came upon either the Moulin Rouge Cabaret or the Louvre Museum.
8. Helena came upon either the Louvre Museum or the Eiffel Tower.
9. Either Betty or Helena came upon St. Peter's Basilica.

	sight in Rome	sight in Paris
Eleanor		
Frances		
Betty		
Helena		

Solution on pages 399–400

P3-22b Orange Pickers

Fruit in the orange groves in a small California area was ready for picking, but there was a shortage of workers to harvest the crops. It was decided that the jobs would be offered to high-school students. The plan was working except that, at the pace the student workers were proceeding, the harvest would be over-ripe before they finished.

As incentive, bonuses were offered, to be given to each of the four fastest pickers based on the amount of fruit picked. The student picking the most oranges would receive the largest bonus; the second, third, and fourth in amount of fruit picked would each receive slightly smaller bonuses. The students quickly finished picking the orange grove, the bonus competition having achieved the desired result.

From the following statements, what were the full names of each of the four pickers receiving bonuses, and in what rank order did they receive them? One of the statements is false.

1. Deek picked more fruit than Bob, who picked more than Chad.

2. Bob did not finish in first or fourth place.
3. Smith, Unger, and Evan said that they never wanted to look at another orange again.
4. Neither Deek nor Chad received the first-place bonus.
5. Evan received second- or third-place bonus money.
6. Bob, who is not Unger, and Evan were so close in the amount of fruit picked that their relative positions had to be settled by a coin toss.
7. Bob was disappointed to receive the bonus amount just below Wagner, although he did get a bigger bonus than Taylor.

	surname	bonus order
Bob		
Chad		
Deek		
Evan		

Solution on page 401

P3-23b **Apartment Dwellers**

In a large city apartment, six inhabitants who live on different floors commute together daily to the same office building. From the statements below, which apartment dweller lives on which of the following floors: the 5th, 10th, 12th, 15th, 17th, and 20th? One of the statements is false.

1. Carl lives three floors above Keith.
2. Keith lives below Kathleen and Kevin.
3. Kathleen lives three floors above Kevin.
4. Cathy lives below Keith and Kathy.
5. Keith lives on the 17th floor.
6. Carl does not live on the 20th floor.
7. Cathy's and Kathy's apartments are five floors apart.

floor

Carl	
Cathy	
Kathleen	
Kathy	
Keith	
Kevin	

Solution on page 402

P3-24b Goldie Locks and the Three Bears

Lincoln Grammar School is preparing to put on their annual first-grade school play. This year it is to be "Goldie Locks and the Three Bears," an updated spoof of the old favorite, and four children have been cast in the well-known parts. From the statements below, one of which is false, determine the full name of each child and the part each student is to play. Two of the children are siblings, so have the same surname. Their first names are no indication of whether any child is male or female or the part they have been cast to play.

1. Mike, Pat, and Del (who was cast as Mama Bear) are not related.
2. Dale and Del, neither of whom got the part of Goldie Locks, met for the first time when they were assigned adjacent desks in school.
3. Mr. and Mrs. Ford were delighted that their son was selected for the part of Papa Bear.
4. Mike and Pat, neither of whom is Foster, live in opposite ends of the school district.

5. Both Pat, who was cast as one of the three bears, and Del are in their first play.
6. The parents of Dale (who is not Farrell) and the Ford boy play bridge together each week.
7. Mike was not happy to be cast as Baby Bear.

	surname	part
Dale		
Del		
Mike		
Pat		

Solution on page 403

P3-25b High-School Basketball Team

The local high-school basketball team is undefeated. This is due primarily to their top six players. One is the center, two are forwards, two are guards, and one is the sixth man who comes off the bench usually before the middle of the first half and, depending on the need, plays either guard or forward. He leads the team in average points scored per game.

One of the following statements is false. Who plays which position?

1. The three seniors are the two forwards and one of the guards.
2. Neither Jerome nor Johnny, who is not a forward, plays the center position; Jake doesn't either.
3. The sixth man is not Jake, who is a sophomore, or Jim.
4. The center is not played by James or by Jim.
5. The position of forward or guard is not played by Joe.

6. The team leader in average points per game is neither Jerome nor Johnny, who is not a forward.
7. Joe is not the center or the sixth man.

position

Jake	
James	
Jerome	
Jim	
Joe	
Johnny	

Solution on page 404

P3-26b State High-School Baseball Championship

Four baseball teams representing four state high schools were in the semifinals for the state championship in their division. The team names were the Bears, the Cardinals, the Lions, and the Wildcats.

Which teams met in the two semifinal games, which two teams won, and which team won the championship? Of the statements below, one is false.

1. The Wildcats and the Bears did not meet in one semifinal game.
2. The Bears did not meet the Cardinals in their semifinal game.
3. The Lions and the Bears did not meet in one semifinal game.
4. The Bears were not in the final game.
5. The team that the Wildcats beat to gain the final was not the Lions.
6. The team that the Lions lost to in their semifinal game won the state championship.

	semi-finals	final game	winner
Bears			
Cardinals			
Lions			
Wildcats			

Solution on pages 405–406

P3-27b Couples' Dinners

Three married couples make it a practice of getting together every Saturday evening for dinner. They take turns meeting at each others' homes.

From the following statements, identify each of the six individuals (one first name is Bert, one surname is Taylor). One of the statements is false.

1. Al and Fran were the couple that instigated the weekly dinners.
2. Eileen and Carl especially enjoy hosting the dinners in their home every third Saturday.
3. Harriet, who is a newlywed, is married either to Carl or Al.
4. Mr. and Mrs. Thomas prefer spicy food. Carl, on the other hand, prefers simple meat-and-potatoes fare.
5. The Thomases have been married the shortest length of time of the three couples.
6. Al and his wife have been married longer than the Tuckers.

	surname
Al	
Bert	
Carl	
Eileen	
Fran	
Harriet	

Solution on pages 406–407

P3-28b Active New Zealand Vacations

Three couples love to vacation in New Zealand and plan to visit there each year. Each couple has a different primary interest that they enjoy. For one couple that interest is the outstanding trekking (hiking) opportunities that the country offers. For a second couple, their primary interest is the world-class fly-fishing. The third couple enjoys some of the more exciting activities available, such as bungee jumping and running river rapids in boats.

What are the full names (one surname is Hart) and primary interest of each couple? One of the statements below is false.

1. June and her husband, Sam, have not tried fly-fishing, nor has Jenny.
2. Holt, Hunt, and their wives like to travel to New Zealand together.
3. The Holts do not live near the other two couples.
4. June and Jenny are neighbors at home.
5. Terry ties his own flies.

6. Kathy and Jenny frequently visit over their common back fence.
7. Sam, who is an experienced trekker, doesn't live near Terry or Patrick.
8. The couple that enjoys fishing takes their vacation during a different month than the other two couples.

	surname	primary interest
Jenny		
June		
Kathy		
Patrick		
Sam		
Terry		

Solution on pages 407–408

P3-29b The Forest People

When the world was young, there lived those known as the Forest People. They were relatively small in stature, and noted for their longevity. From the statements below, determine the heights and ages of five of these individuals. Their heights, measured in hands, were twelve, thirteen, fourteen, fifteen, and sixteen hands. Their ages were 100, 110, 120, 130, and 140 years. One statement is false.

1. Har was not the oldest, nor was he the shortest or the tallest.
2. Winn was taller than Edvo, who was taller but younger than Frer.
3. Tolo, who was not the second oldest, was older than Har, and shorter than Frer.
4. The one who was thirteen hands tall was looked up to as the oldest.
5. Har was taller and older than Winn and Tolo.
6. The fourth oldest was taller than Tolo, but shorter than Edvo, who was older than Winn.

	Edvo	Frer	Har	Tolo	Winn
hands tall 12					
13					
14					
15					
16					
ages 100					
110					
120					
130					
140					

Solution on pages 408–409

P3-30b Tree Plantings

In one block in town there are five homes on one side of the street. The five neighbors decided that the town needed more trees. With the support of the Town Council, they agreed that they would each plant several trees in public areas, as well as on their own properties. Each planted several of one variety of tree, and each of the five neighbors planted a different variety.

From the statements that follow, determine the full names of each neighbor, and the variety of tree that each planted. One statement is false.

1. Jacobs lives to the immediate right of Ken and to the immediate left of Doug.
2. Ted was going to plant quaking aspens, but he found out that was the variety the neighbor on his immediate right (who was not Doug) had selected.
3. Art, who is not Jacobs, planted white oaks.
4. Gene is not Jacobs or West, nor does he live next door to either of them.
5. Doug did not plant the water birches.

6. Neither the blue spruces nor bigleaf maples were planted by Art.
7. Bagnall's first name is not Ted.
8. Waldron's home is at the right end of the block; he planted white oaks; Ken's home is not at the left end of the block.
9. Egan, who lives next door to Art, on one side, and Gene, on the other, did not plant bigleaf maples.
10. Art does not live on the right end of the block.

	surname	trees planted
Art		
Doug		
Gene		
Ken		
Ted		

Solution on pages 409–411

The C's

The following puzzles each contain a number of statements, each of which provides a piece of information, as did the puzzles in the previous two parts. However, the statements within each puzzle in this part are false, excepting only one statement which is true. Your challenge in solving these puzzles is to first identify the true statement.

NOTE: If any part of a statement is false, the entire statement is false.

P3-31c Golfers' Handicaps

Four friends play golf together regularly; their handicaps are 14, 18, 22, and 26.

From the statements below, which golfer has which handicap? Three of the statements are false; only one is true.

1. Alice has either the lowest or the next to the lowest handicap.
2. Carol's handicap is higher than Alice's and lower than Diane's.
3. Beth's handicap is the highest.
4. Diane's handicap is higher than either Alice's or Carol's.

handicap

	14	18	22	26
Alice				
Beth				
Carol				
Diane				

Solution on pages 411–412

P3-32c Football Players

The Central High School football team is undefeated. They depend heavily on their four star players. One is the quarterback, one is a wide receiver, and two are running backs.

From the statements below, what is the position played by each of these four star players? Only one statement is true; the others are false.

1. If, and only if, Charley is not one of the running backs, then Mike is the quarterback.
2. Buddy is the quarterback.
3. Mike and Jamey are not the two running backs.
4. The wide receiver is either Charley or Buddy.

	position played
Buddy	
Charley	
Jamey	
Mike	

Solution on pages 412–414

P3-33c Cloud Formations

One summer day, four children lay resting on a lawn. One noticed a cloud formation that looked like a flock of sheep. Another saw a rabbit; a third saw a lion; and the fourth spotted a cloud alligator.

From the following statements, of which only one is true, which child saw which animal (or animals) in the clouds?

1. Charlie did not see either an alligator or a rabbit.
2. Either Diane or Charlie saw a lion.
3. Becky did not see the flock of sheep until it was pointed out to her by one of the other children.
4. One of Andy and Diane spotted an alligator and the other spotted a flock of sheep.

	cloud formation
Andy	
Becky	
Charlie	
Diane	

Solution on pages 414–416

P3-34c Puzzle Challenges

Four friends enjoy the challenge of solving puzzles, although each favors a different kind. One prefers crossword puzzles, one prefers jigsaw puzzles, one prefers logic puzzles, and one prefers mathematical puzzles.

From the statements below, determine who prefers which kind of puzzle. Only one statement is true; the others are false.

1. Bill prefers either mathematical puzzles or crossword puzzles, and Bea favors jigsaw puzzles.
2. Either Barney or Betty prefers logic puzzles.
3. Jigsaw puzzles are preferred by Betty, Bea, or Bill.
4. Either Betty or Bill prefers logic puzzles; the other prefers mathematical puzzles.
5. Either crossword puzzles or mathematical puzzles are preferred by Barney.

	puzzles preferred
Barney	
Bea	
Betty	
Bill	

Solution on pages 416–417

P3-35c Golf Tournament Winners

Three winners in three different flights in the Mountain Golf Club tournament were Bill, Charlie, and Dan. The players were grouped into three flights according to their handicap. One of them won the A flight, one won the B flight, and one won the C flight.

From the statements below, which golfer won which flight? Only one of the statements is true; the others are false.

1. Bill won the A flight and Dan won the B flight.
2. Charlie won the C flight.
3. Bill did not win the C flight.
4. The A flight was not won by either Charlie or Dan.

	flight A	flight B	flight C
Bill	✕		✕
Dan		✕	
Charlie			✕

Bill   B
Dan   C
Charlie A

Solution on pages 418–419

P3-36c Four Vocations

Four neighbors, Mr. Baker, Mr. Butcher, Mr. Cook, and Mr. Carpenter, are a baker, a butcher, a cook, and a carpenter, although none is employed in the vocation that is his namesake. Can you determine the vocation of each of the four?

Four of the statements below are false; only one is true.

1. Mr. Carpenter is the baker.
2. Neither Mr. Butcher nor Mr. Baker is the cook.
3. The butcher is neither Mr. Baker nor Mr. Carpenter.
4. Mr. Cook is the carpenter.
5. Mr. Butcher is the baker.

	vocation			
	baker	butcher	carpenter	cook
Mr. Baker				
Mr. Butcher				
Mr. Carpenter				
Mr. Cook				

Solution on pages 419–420

P3-37c Friends and Cats

Three good friends, who love cats, have each named their cat after one of the other friends. Of the clues that follow, only one is true; the others are false.

Which friend owns which cat?

1. Candy's cat is named either Dody or Alice.
2. Betsy's cat is named Alice.
3. Either the cat named Candy or the cat named Betsy is owned by Dody.
4. Neither the cat named Betsy nor the cat named Candy belongs to Alice.
5. The cat named Dody does not belong to Candy or Betsy.

	cat
Alice	
Betsy	
Candy	
Dody	

Solution on pages 421–422

P3-38c The Mountaintop Hermits

Four brothers decided years ago that a hermit's life was for them. The world had gotten too fast and complicated, what with internal combustion engines, wireless communications, and people telling you what to do.

They settled in a mountain range in the Southwest, and each built a shelter on a separate mountaintop. One shelter faced north, one south, one east, and one west. They agreed to get together to share experiences on a regular basis. They met at one brother's shelter every spring, a second brother's shelter every summer, the third shelter every fall, and the fourth shelter every winter.

From the several statements below, which brother settled on which mountaintop, and what season of the year did they meet at each brother's shelter?

Only one of the following statements is true.

1. Billy's shelter did not face south, nor was his shelter the location for the winter meetings.
2. Their summer meetings were not at the shelter that faced north or the shelter that faced south.

3. Homer hosted the fall, winter, or summer meetings, and either he or Billy lived in the shelter that faced east and the other lived in the shelter that faced west.

4. Either Jacob or Willy, whose shelter faced west, hosted the summer meetings.

5. The fall meetings were hosted by Jacob, whose shelter faced south.

	shelter direction	host season
Billy		
Homer		
Jacob		
Willy		

Solution on pages 422–424

P3-39c Sailboat Race

Five couples enjoy sailboating, and they get together frequently to race each other. On one such occasion, two of their boats finished the race in a dead heat for first place, with the other three boats close behind.

From the following clues, which two finished in a tie for first place and which boats finished third, fourth, and fifth? One statement is true; the others are false.

1. The Steinbergs were neither one of the two who finished in a dead heat for first place, nor the couple who finished in third place.
2. The Stanfords finished immediately behind the two who tied for first place.
3. The Stewarts did not finish either ahead of the Stanfords or behind the Smiths.
4. The Smiths finished two places ahead of the Stanfords, and immediately behind the two first-place finishers.
5. The Standfords did not finish in either fourth place or fifth place.
6. The Stahls finished ahead of both the Smiths and the Steinbergs.

	finish place
Smiths	
Stahls	
Stanfords	
Steinbergs	
Stewarts	

Solution on pages 424–426

P3-40c Jazz Combo

A jazz group plays three nights a week at Johnny's Seven Seas Restaurant. There are five members of the band: a tenor saxophone player, a piano player, a guitar player, a string bass player, and a drummer.

From the statements that follow, only one of which is true, who plays which instrument?

1. The saxophone player frequently receives requests to play "*Crazy Rhythm*," which is one of her favorites.
2. Steve plays neither the piano nor the bass.
3. The guitar man is neither Al nor Ansel, who doesn't play the piano.
4. Ansel does not play the guitar, the piano, or the bass.
5. The drums are not played by Caroline, Ansel, or Roger.
6. The saxophone is not played by Roger or Al.
7. The drums are played by Steve, Ansel, or Al.

	instrument
Ansel	
Caroline	
Al	
Roger	
Steve	

Solution on pages 426–428

4.

Hyperborea

Hyperborea was a most wondrous land. According to Herodotus, the first-known ancient world historian, Hyperborea was located in that part of the world north of Mount Olympus, home of the gods, and the inhabitants were much favored by the gods. The Hyperboreans were fortunate to live in a land of continual springtime. There was no disease, and the people lived for a thousand years. These things are known.

What is not well known are the unusual standards of veracity by which the people lived. Those who lived in the southern region were known as Sororeans. They always spoke truthfully. Those who lived in the northern region were known as Nororeans, and they always spoke falsely. Hyperboreans who lived in the middle region were known as Midroreans, and they made statements that were alternately truthful and false, or false and truthful.

These puzzles are about the Hyperboreans and their standards of veracity.

P4-1 Which Road to Take

The Hyperboreans were especially favored by the god Apollo, who visited them in disguise. Apollo wished to establish a meaningful dialogue with the inhabitants, but that was not easily accomplished.

Apollo, walking along, meets two inhabitants at a fork in the road, one road going to the left and the other to the right. The two Hyperboreans are known to be a Sororean, who always speaks truthfully, and a Nororean, who always speaks falsely. But which one is which?

Apollo inquires as to which road he should take. The first inhabitant responds as follows:

A. Take the road to the left.

Apollo, still a little uncertain, speaks to the first inhabitant again, and asks: "If I ask B which road to take, what will he say?"

A. B will say to take the road to the left.

Which one of A and B is the Sororean, which one is the Nororean, and which road should Apollo take?

	Sororean	Nororean
A		
B		

Indicate + (plus) or − (minus) in the diagram above as you draw conclusions regarding the veracity of the two Hyperboreans.

Solution on page 429

P4-2 Apollo Goes down the Road

A little confused, Apollo takes one of the two roads and meets two more inhabitants. This time he inquires as to the standard, or standards, of veracity of the two Hyperboreans. Sororeans always speak truthfully; Nororeans always speak falsely; and Midroreans make statements that are alternately truthful and false, or false and truthful. As to the group or groups to which these two speakers belong, little is known. They each make two responses:

A. 1. I am a Nororean.
    2. Neither of us is a Sororean.

B. 1. I am a Sororean.
    2. A is a Nororean.

What group or groups do A and B represent?

	A	B
1		
2		
Sororean		
Nororean		
Midrorean		

Consider each statement and, as you draw conclusions, indicate + (plus) or − (minus) in the diagram.

Solution on page 430

P4-3 Some Just Like to Be Difficult

Maybe Apollo needs to be more insistent. He does not seem to be making any headway at understanding the inhabitants. He decides to change his approach.

He meets three Hyperboreans and, with maybe a little less tact than he should use, he inquires as to their group or groups. Hyperboreans belong to different groups: Sororeans, who always speak truthfully; Nororeans, who always speak falsely; and Midroreans, who make statements that are alternately truthful and false, or false and truthful. As to these three, little is known as to their group or groups.

They respond as follows:

A. 1. I am not a Sororean.
   2. C is a Midrorean.

B. 1. I am not a Nororean.
   2. A is a Sororean.

C. 1. I am not a Midrorean.
   2. B is a Nororean.

Which group or groups are represented by the three speakers?

	A	B	C
1			
2			
Sororean			
Nororean			
Midrorean			

Solution on page 430–431

P4-4 One Speaks Truthfully

Apollo, still trying to establish meaningful communication with the Hyperboreans, this time meets three more inhabitants. They are known as a Sororean, who always speaks truthfully; a Nororean, who always speaks falsely; and a Midrorean, who makes statements that are alternately truthful and false. Apollo now asks each of them which one is from which region. Their answers follow:

A. 1. C is the Nororean.
   2. B is not the Sororean.

B. 1. C is not the Sororean.
   2. A is the Nororean.

C. 1. B is the Midrorean.
   2. I am not the Nororean.

Which speaker represents which region?

	A	B	C
1			
2			
Sororean			
Nororean			
Midrorean			

Solution on pages 431–432

P4-5 Apollo Makes One Last Try

Apollo is ready to return to Mount Olympus, but he is willing to make one last try at establishing meaningful dialogue with the Hyperboreans. He approaches three inhabitants, who are known to be a Sororean, who always speaks truthfully; a Nororean, who always speaks falsely; and a Midrorean, who makes statements that are alternately truthful and false.

Apollo reasons that he needs to find out which one is the Sororean, so he asks that question. The inhabitants don't, however, seem to be very cooperative. Two respond as below, and one of the three doesn't feel like talking:

- A. 1. Neither C nor I are the Midrorean.
  2. B is the Nororean.
  3. B's second statement is true.

- B. 1. I am not the Nororean.
  2. C is the Midrorean.

- C. (no response)

Which one is the Sororean, which one is the Nororean, and which one is the Midrorean?

	A	B	C
1			
2			
3			
Sororean			
Nororean			
Midrorean			

Solution on pages 432–433

P4-6 Who Extracts the Sunflower Seeds?

Three inhabitants are discussing their occupations, which are all different, in response to a visitor's inquiry. As to their groups, little is known except that none of them is a Sororean. Therefore, the speakers are Nororeans, who always speak falsely, and/or Midroreans, who make statements that are alternately truthful and false.

What group or groups are represented by the three speakers, and what are their occupations?

A. 1. My job as the sunflower-seed extractor is the most favorable occupation.
   2. C's second statement is false.
   3. B is not the shepherd.

B. 1. A is the olive processor.
   2. I am not a Midrorean.

C. 1. A and B are both shepherds.
   2. I am the sunflower-seed extractor.

	A	B	C
1			
2			
3			
Nororean			
Midrorean			
occupation			

Solution on page 433

P4-7 The Delegation of Centaurs

Centaurs, who were half human and half horse, lived on Mount Pelion, which was south of Mount Olympus. The centaurs thought it would be nice to establish friendly relationships with the Hyperborean people so they sent a delegation to Hyperborea to open communications.

The centaur delegation approaches three Hyperboreans and attempts to engage them in conversation. The three Hyperboreans are known to be a Sororean, who always speaks truthfully; a Nororean, who always speaks falsely; and a Midrorean, who makes statements that are alternately truthful and false.

From their statements, which Hyperborean belongs to which group?

A. 1. B is less truthful than I.
    2. C is less truthful than B.

B. 1. A is more truthful than C.
    2. C is less truthful than I.

C. 1. I am not the Midrorean.
    2. A's second statement is false.

The group of centaurs realizes the futility of their mission, and they return to Mount Pelion.

	A	B	C
1			
2			
Sororean			
Nororean			
Midrorean			

Solution on page 434

P4-8 The Story of Pelops

There is an ancient Greek story, reportedly true, about a prince named Pelops who tampered with the wheel of his racing rival's chariot. The wheel came off at the first turn of the race, and Pelops won. Actually, the incident happened not in Greece, but in Hyperborea. Pelops was a visitor during the first Olympic Games (which occurred in Hyperborea). When he was exposed as a schemer, he quickly left and returned to Greece, where he was treated as a hero, and a region, the Peloponnessus, was named after him.

Four Hyperboreans are discussing the incident. The four are a Sororean, who always speaks truthfully, two Nororeans, who always speak falsely, and a Midrorean, who makes statements that are alternately truthful and false, or false and truthful. Which of the speakers represent which groups?

A. 1. Pelops is a Nororean.
   2. C is not a Nororean.

B. 1. I sent Pelops back to Greece.
   2. A is a Nororean.

C. 1. I am not a Nororean.
   2. B did not send Pelops back to Greece.

D. 1. I didn't like Pelops when I first saw him.
   2. B is not a Nororean.

	A	B	C	D
1				
2				
Sororean				
Nororean				
Midrorean				

Solution on page 435

P4-9 Who's Older?

Hyperboreans often live for a thousand years. Four inhabitants are discussing their ages, which are 100, 200, 300, and 400 years. One is a Sororean, known to always speak truthfully, and three are Midroreans, who make statements that are alternately truthful and false. Their statements follow:

A. 1. I am the oldest among us.
   2. I am the Sororean.
   3. C is younger than D.

B. 1. C is the youngest among us.
   2. B and D are 100 years apart in age.

C. 1. I am older than A.
   2. B is a hundred years older than D.

D: 1. C is not older than A.
   2. I am older than B.

What is the group and age of each speaker?

	A	B	C	D
1				
2				
3				
Sororean				
Midrorean				
age				

Solution on pages 436–437

P4-10 The Game of Golf

It is a little-known fact that the game of golf was invented in Hyperborea many years before it was rediscovered in Scotland. Three Hyperboreans are discussing the sport with a visitor.

Hyperboreans fall into three groups: Sororeans, who always speak truthfully; Nororeans, who always speak falsely; and Midroreans, who make statements that are alternately truthful and false. As to the group or groups of these particular speakers, little is known except that at least one is a Nororean. Their statements follow:

A. 1. We have been playing golf for well over a hundred years.
   2. I am not a Nororean.
   3. I am president of the Hyperborean Golf Association.

B. 1. I invented the game of golf.
   2. I always speak the truth.
   3. A's third statement is true.

C. 1. B did not invent the game of golf.
  2. I am not a Midrorean.
  3. One of us is a Midrorean.
  4. We Hyperboreans have been playing golf for less than a hundred years.

What group or groups are represented by these speakers?

	A	B	C
1			
2			
3			
4			
Sororean			
Nororean			
Midrorean			

Solution on pages 437–438

P4-11 Sunflowers Galore

Hyperborea exists in perpetual springtime. Fields of flowers continually in bloom are enjoyed at all times by the inhabitants. They especially enjoy sunflowers, whose tasty seeds and oil are valuable to all, and they delight in the beautiful sunflower blossoms.

Four inhabitants of the land are discussing the sunflowers and why they are so special. Hyperboreans belong to three groups: Sororeans always speak truthfully, Nororeans always speak falsely, and Midroreans make statements that are alternately truthful and false.

To which group or groups do these four speakers belong?

A. 1. We love to eat sunflower seeds.
   2. We all belong to the same group.

B. 1. Sunflower oil makes the flowers valuable to us.
   2. We each belong to a different group.

C. 1. Sunflower seeds and oil are not valuable to us.
   2. A's second statement is true.

D. 1. B's second statement is true.
   2. A's second statement is also true.
   3. Sunflowers are overrated; they give most
      of us hay fever.

	A	B	C	D
1				
2				
3				
Sororean				
Nororean				
Midrorean				

Solution on pages 438–439

P4-12 Who's an Outlier?

In any group of people you can expect to find a few who don't adhere to the conventions accepted by the majority. In this, Hyperboreans are no exception.

There are a few individuals who actually disdain the Hyperboreans' three standards of veracity. They are not Sororeans, who always speak truthfully; Nororeans, who always speak falsely; or Midroreans, who make statements that are alternately truthful and false. They are Hyperborea's Outliers. These inhabitants' statement patterns as to truth and falseness are anything that is different. Therefore, their statements here are, in some order, either two truthful statements in sequence then one false statement, or one truthful statement then two false statements.

Following are statements made by inhabitants, discussing their involvement in the first Olympic Games. One is known to be a Sororean; one is known to be a Nororean; one is known to be a Midrorean; and one is known to be an Outlier. Which is which?

A. 1. B is the Outlier.
   2. I finished in first place in the discus throw.
   3. There is another Olympic Games scheduled for next year.

B. 1. Who's an Outlier? I'm not an Outlier.
   2. A is the Sororean.
   3. A was next to last in the discuss throw.

C. 1. I am the Outlier.
   2. I entered every event.
   3. A's third statement is false.

D. 1. A's first statement is false.
   2. A's third statement is true.
   3. C did not enter any of the events.

	A	B	C	D
1				
2				
3				
Sororean				
Nororean				
Midrorean				
Outlier				

Solution on pages 439–440

P4-13 Who's Grumbling?

Hyperboreans lived in ideal conditions. Theirs was a land of almost-perpetual sunshine—a perfect environment for their valuable sunflower crop—and abundance. However, a few people can always be counted on to find reasons to complain, as can be observed in the following discussion by four inhabitants. Hyperboreans are known to be Sororeans, who always speak truthfully; Nororeans, who always speak falsely; Midroreans, who make statements that are alternately truthful and false; and Outliers, whose standard of veracity is anything that does not agree with the three traditional Hyperborean standards.

As to the group or groups of the speakers below, one and only one is known to be a Midrorean and one and only one is known to be an Outlier. Little is known of the group or groups of the other two.

A. 1. I saw some snow once; I wish it would snow.
   2. D is a Nororean.
   3. I am not the Midrorean.

B. 1. A good windstorm would be a change, and would help the sunflower crop.

2. A has never seen snow.
3. I am a Nororean.

C. 1. A is not the Midrorean.
   2. A has never seen snow.
   3. A windstorm would not help the sunflower crop.

D. 1. C is not the Outlier.
   2. Neither A nor I have seen snow.
   3. I am not a Nororean.

	A	B	C	D
I				
2				
3				
Sororean				
Nororean				
Midrorean				
Outlier				

Solution on pages 440-441

P4-14 The Hunt for an Aspidochelon

To catch an aspidochelon, four strong fishermen must throw a huge net over it—then hang on for dear life! At least that's the theory. No one has ever seen one, much less caught one. The aspidochelon is a gigantic sea monster rumored to be a gastronomical delicacy.

Four big husky fishermen, determined to be the first to catch an aspidochelon, set out to sea. As to their groups, two are Nororeans; who always speak falsely; one is a Midrorean; who makes statements that are alternately truthful and false; and one is an Outlier, whose statements are anything that is not acceptable Hyperborean veracity. The four fishermen discuss this exciting challenge among themselves, below:

A. 1. I packed lots of food and juice for the hunt.
   2. We have been at sea long enough to see our quarry.
   3. D is small and weak; he should not be on this hunt.

B. 1. A is the lead fisherman for this trip because he has seen an aspidochelon.

2. C's second statement is true.
3. A's first statement is true.

C. 1. A packed plenty of grape juice, but not much food for our hunt.
   2. I am the lead fisherman, because I have seen an aspidochelon.
   3. We have not been at sea long enough to see our quarry.

D. 1. None of us has ever seen an aspidochelon.
   2. All of B's statements are true.
   3. C's third statement is false.

	A	B	C	D
1				
2				
3				
Nororean				
Midrorean				
Outlier				

Solution on pages 442–443

P4-15 Return from the Aspidochelon Hunt

A crowd gathered on shore as four very tired fishermen returned from their hunt for the giant sea monster called an aspidochelon. Of the four fishermen, one is a Midrorean, who makes statements that are alternately truthful and false; two are Nororeans, who always speak falsely; and one is an Outlier, whose statements are not consistent with traditional Hyperborean standards of veracity. Their statements follow:

A. 1. We saw an aspidochelon; we really did.
    2. C makes only false statements.
    3. I did not get my blisters from rowing.

B. 1. What we saw in the distance was not
        an aspidochelon; it was an island.
    2. I did not fall overboard.
    3. I am not a Nororean.

C. 1. A's second statement is true.
    2. B fell overboard.
    3. I am not a Nororean.

D. 1. A did not get his blisters from rowing.
   2. B did not fall overboard.
   3. I am not a Nororean.

Which fisherman is the Midrorean, which are the Nororeans, and which is the Outlier?

	A	B	C	D
1				
2				
3				
Nororean				
Midrorean				
Outlier				

Solution on pages 443–444

P4-16 Two Outliers

Traditions tend to weaken over time. At least it seems so. At any rate, Hyperborea is seeing more Outliers.

The five speakers below are discussing the Olympic Games recently concluded. The five are known to be a Sororean, who always speaks truthfully; a Nororean, who always speaks falsely; a Midrorean, who makes statements that are alternately truthful and false; and two Outliers, whose standards of veracity are different than the other three speakers.

A. 1. I would have participated, if the athletes wore loincloths.
   2. B is not the Sororean.
   3. D did not win the gold medal.
   4. C would have won the gold medal, except for his sunburn.

B. 1. E won the silver medal.
   2. C's first statement is false.
   3. C did not win a medal.
   4. E is either the Midrorean or an Outlier.

C. 1. I am not the Midrorean.
   2. I would not have won the gold medal
      even if I didn't have my sunburn.
   3. B did not win the bronze medal.
   4. B is the Sororean.

NOTE: D and E speakers on next page.

	A	B	C	D	E
1					
2					
3					
4					
Sororean					
Nororean					
Midrorean					
Outlier					
medal					

D. 1. I won the gold medal.
   2. B did not win the bronze medal.
   3. A would have participated if the athletes wore loincloths.
   4. C is not the Nororean.

E. 1. I won the gold medal.
   2. C wouldn't have won the gold medal even without his sunburn.
   3. I am not the Sororean.
   4. A would have participated if the athletes wore loincloths.

Which speaker is the Sororean, which is the Nororean, which is the Midrorean, which two are Outliers, and who won the medals?

Solution on pages 444–446

P4-17 Apollo Meets an Outlier

The Hyperboreans are favored by Apollo, but he has not had any success in establishing meaningful dialogue with the inhabitants. He is aware that there are those among the Hyperboreans who do not respect their traditional conventions regarding veracity. Perhaps he might have better luck making contact with an Outlier.

Apollo, in disguise, approaches four inhabitants, exactly one of whom is known to be an Outlier, whose standard of veracity is different than that of Sororeans, who always speak truthfully; Nororeans, who always speak falsely; and Midroreans, who make statements that are alternately truthful and false. As to the group or groups of the other three speakers, little is known except that no more than one is a Sororean.

Apollo asks which one of the four is the Outlier. They each respond below:

A. 1. Two of us are Outliers.
   2. B is a Sororean.
   3. B was an Outlier, but he has reformed.
   4. B's third statement is true.

B. 1. I am neither a Nororean nor a Midrorean.
   2. A's first statement is true.
   3. D is a Sororean and C is the Outlier.
   4. A is not the Outlier.

C. 1. D is a Sororean.
   2. I am the Outlier.
   3. B's second statement is false.
   4. D is neither a Sororean nor a Midrorean.

D. 1. B is either a Midrorean or the Outlier.
   2. I am either a Sororean or a Midrorean.
   3. C falsely claims to be the Outlier.
   4. A's third statement is false.

Apollo throws up his hands in frustration. It is time, he decides, for him to give up and return to Mount Olympus to try to forget about the Hyperboreans.

What group is represented by the each of the four speakers?

	A	B	C	D
1				
2				
3				
4				
Sororean				
Nororean				
Midrorean				
Outlier				

Solution on pages 446–447

5.
Letters for Digits

In the addition and subtraction problems in this section, digits have been replaced by letters. You will find three kinds of puzzles. They are as follows:

A's: In these puzzles, each letter represents the same digit wherever it occurs in the given puzzle.

B's: In the puzzles in this second part, each letter represents the same digit wherever it occurs in the given mathematical *problem*, that is, *above the line*. Wherever a letter appears in the *answer* to the problem, that is, *below the line*, it represents a digit that is one more than or one less than the same letter above the line. For example, if B equals 4 above the line, all B's below the line will be equal to either 3 or 5.

C's: The puzzles in this part are similar to those in part B, except that the digits are unknown.

P5-1a Subtraction, Three Digits

Each digit has been replaced by a letter. Each letter represents the same digit wherever it occurs. The digits are 0, 4, and 8.

$$
\begin{array}{r}
A\ C\ A \\
-\ C\ C\ C \\
\hline
C\ B\ C
\end{array}
$$

Determine the digit represented by each letter.

Solution on pages 448–449

P5-2a Addition, Four Digits

Each digit has been replaced by a letter. Each letter represents the same digit wherever it occurs. The digits are 1, 2, 3, and 4.

```
    A A
 +  B C
    C D
```

Identify the digit represented by each letter.

Solution on pages 449–450

P5-3a Subtraction, Four Digits

Each letter represents the same digit wherever it occurs in the puzzle. The digits are 2, 4, 6, and 8.

```
    A B C
 -  B D B
    D D B
```

What digit is represented by each letter?

Solution on pages 450–451

P5-4a Addition, Five Digits

Each letter in this addition problem represents the same digit wherever it occurs. The digits are 1, 2, 3, 4, and 5.

```
    A A E
+   E A C
    B D D
```

Determine the digit represented by each letter.

Solution on page 451

P5-5a Addition, Six Digits

Each letter in this addition problem represents the same digit wherever it occurs. The digits are 0, 2, 3, 4, 5, and 6.

```
    A E A C A
+   E E A B D
    F C D C C
```

What digit is represented by each letter?

Solution on page 452

P5-6a Addition, Six Digits Again

Each letter stands for the same digit wherever it occurs. The digits are 0, 1, 3, 5, 7, and 9.

```
    B C E C
  + E C E F
  ─────────
  A E E A D
```

What does each letter stand for?

Solution on page 453

P5-7a Subtraction, Five Digits

Each letter represents a digit wherever it occurs in the puzzle. The digits are 2, 3, 5, 7, and 9.

```
    A C E
  - C E D
  ───────
  F F F
```

Determine the digit represented by each letter.

Solution on pages 454–455

P5-8a Addition, Eight Digits

Each letter has been substituted for one of the eight digits. The digits are 0, 1, 2, 3, 4, 5, 6, and 7.

```
    C D A F C
  + C D C B H
  H E C E G F
```

What digit is represented by each letter?

Solution on pages 455–456

P5-9a Addition, Eight Digits Again

Each letter stands for the same digit wherever it occurs. The digits are 2, 3, 4, 5, 6, 7, 8, and 9.

```
        B C
    E E F E C
    E H D H A
  + H E A E H
    F G G B H
```

Determine the digit represented by each letter.

Solution on pages 457–458

P5-10a Addition, Seven Digits

Each letter represents the same digit wherever it occurs. The digits are 1, 2, 3, 4, 5, 7, and 8.

```
    G D B E G A
    D D F B A A
  + D G C B A A
  ─────────────
  A E G A B C G
```

What does each letter stand for?

Solution on pages 458–459

P5-11b Subtraction, Four Digits Again

Each letter above the line represents a digit that has a difference of one from the digit represented by the same letter below the line. The digits are 0, 1, 2, and 3.

```
    B  B  A
 -  A  C  A
    A  B  C
```

What digit or digits are represented by each letter?

Solution on pages 459–460

P5-12b Addition, Five Digits Again

Each letter above the line represents a digit with a difference of one from the digit represented by the same letter below the line. The digits are 2, 3, 5, 6, and 7.

```
    D D B E
  + E A E B
    C B D A
```

What digit or digits does each letter represent?

Solution on pages 460–461

P5-13b Subtraction, Five Digits Again

Each letter above the line in this subtraction problem represents a digit that has a difference of one from the digit represented by the same letter below the line. The digits are 0, 1, 2, 3, and 5.

```
    A A D A
  - E E C E
    D B F D
```

What digit or digits does each letter represent?

Solution on page 462

P5-14b Addition, Seven Digits Again

Each letter above the line represents a digit that has a difference of one from the digit represented by the same letter below the line. The digits are 0, 1, 2, 4, 6, 7, and 8.

```
    A D A E
  + F C D E
    A D E E
  E F D C F
```

What digit or digits are represented by each letter?

Solution on pages 463–464

P5-15b Addition, Seven Digits Once Again

Each letter above the line represents a digit that has a difference of one from the digit represented by the same letter below the line. The digits are 0, 1, 2, 3, 4, 5, and 9.

```
    E E C C C
    E E E E F E
  + E E E D B D
  ─────────────
    A B F A B A
```

What digit or digits are represented by each letter?

Solution on pages 464–465

P5-16c Subtraction, Three Unknown Digits

There are only three digits. The digits are unknown.

$$
\begin{array}{r}
A\ B \\
-\ A\ A \\
\hline
A\ B
\end{array}
$$

What digit or digits are represented by each letter?

Solution on page 466

253

P5-17c Subtraction, Four Unknown Digits

Each letter in the puzzle below represents the same digit wherever it occurs in the mathematical problem (above the line). Wherever a letter appears in the answer to the problem (below the line) it represents one number different from the digit represented by the same letter above the line. The four digits are unknown.

$$
\begin{array}{r}
\text{A B A A C} \\
- \ \text{A C C A A} \\
\hline
\text{A A B C}
\end{array}
$$

What digit or digits does each letter represent?

Solution on pages 466–467

P5-18c Addition, Five Unknown Digits

Each letter above the line represents a digit that has a difference of one from the digit represented by the same letter below the line. There are only five digits. The digits are unknown.

```
    A C D A
  + A C A A
  ---------
    C B A C
```

What digit or digits are represented by each letter?

Solution on pages 468–469

P5-19c Addition, Five Unknown Digits Again

Finally, here again, each letter above the line represents a digit one number different from the digit represented by the same letter below the line. There are five unknown digits.

```
    A D A B A
  + C A C B A
  ─────────────
    D B A B C
```

What digit or digits are represented by each letter?

Solution on pages 469–470

6.
Desert Foothills Golf

A nine-hole desert golf course was designed by a highly regarded but very eccentric genius who went a bit over the hill" in designing it. The course is reportedly very challenging. However, the challenge is not so much the difficulty of the golf course as it is of finding your way from each green to the next tee. It seems there's the matter of mountain lions, rattlesnakes, gila monsters, scorpions, and spiny cactus at virtually every step away from the fairways and greens, in addition to the desert heat and lack of water, so many an unaware golfer has met with severe misfortune.

P6-1 The First Decision

A lone vacationing golfer happens upon a sign advertising challenging desert foothills golf, and he accepts its challenge. There appears to be nothing especially challenging about the first hole. The fairway is straight and flat, and there appear to be no obstacles; he is a little disappointed.

The situation changes when he leaves the green and looks for the second tee. No tee is within sight. What he finds are two paths with a sign posted at each. In reading the scorecard, he finds a reference to paths that lead the golfer from each green to the next tee. It states:

> "Directional signs indicate the correct paths."

In small print, a notation states that at least one of the signs to the second tee is false. He inspects the two signs (shown on the next page).

A

> This is the
> path to the
> second tee.

B

> These signs
> are both true.

Which path should be taken?

	sign A	sign B
If path A		
If path B		

Assume each path in turn is the path to take. Indicate
T (for True) or F (for False) near sign A and sign B in
each case.

Solution on page 472

P6-2 The Second Decision

The golfer manages to select the correct path and before long he is playing the second hole. This time, on leaving the green, he sees not two but three paths, one of which is purported to lead to the second tee. Three signs, one at each path, are his clues.

He again consults his scorecard and reads that the correct decision could conclusively be made. The path signs are below:

A
Exactly two
of these signs
are false.

B
This path
leads to the
third tee.

C
This is
the right
path to
take.

Which path should the golfer select?

	sign A	sign B	sign C
If path A			
If path B			
If path C			

Solution on page 473

P6-3 The Third Decision

Again, he makes the right decision, but so far the golf course doesn't seem very appealing. He plays the third hole and, as anticipated, encounters three more paths with accompanying signs. His scorecard, in barely discernible print, states that only one of the three signs is true. He reads the signs, as follows:

A
> The sign at
> path B is
> false.

B
> Follow this
> path to the
> fourth tee.

C
> This path
> is not the way to
> the fourth tee.

Which path should be taken?

	sign A	sign B	sign C
If path A			
If path B			
If path C			

Solution on page 474

P6-4 The Fourth Decision

After arriving safely at the fourth tee and playing the hole, the golfer prepares himself for what he knows will be another challenge that is not nearly as much fun as golf. He sees three more paths, with a sign next to each, and only one leads to the fifth tee. His scorecard says that at least one sign is false. He reads the signs as follows:

A
Path B is correct, or else path C is.

B
If, and only if, this path is not correct, then path C is.

C
Either this path or path B is correct.

Which is the correct path?

	sign A	sign B	sign C
If path A			
If path B			
If path C			

Solution on page 475

P6-5 The Fifth Decision

The fifth hole isn't much fun, since he is thinking too much about the next set of signs. After completing the fifth hole, he is confronted by three more paths and their signs. According to the fine print in his scorecard, exactly one of the signs is false. He reads them as follows:

A
> Path C leads
> to the
> 6th tee.

B
> Take this
> path to the
> 6th tee.

C
> This path
> leads to the
> open desert.

Which path should the golfer take?

	sign A	sign B	sign C
If path A			
If path B			
If path C			

Solution on page 476

P6-6 The Sixth Decision

Once again the golfer's reasoning is correct. Those beads of perspiration aren't from the heat, though. He plays the sixth hole without much enthusiasm, and approaches the next set of paths, hoping to get safely to the seventh tee.

His scorecard says that exactly one of the signs is false. He reads the signs, below:

A
> Path B is
> not the way
> to go.

B
> Take this
> path to the
> 7th tee.

C
> Sign A is false.

Which path should be taken?

	sign A	sign B	sign C
If path A			
If path B			
If path C			

Solution on page 477

P6-7 The Seventh Decision

The golfer has made several correct decisions and is gaining in confidence. Perhaps now he can manage to concentrate on his golf game. He plays well at the seventh hole, and approaches the next set of signs without quite as much nervousness. He consults his scorecard, which indicates that the sign at the path to take is the only false sign. His confidence evaporates. The signs are as follows:

A
> The sign at path B is the false sign.

B
> This is not the path to take.

C
> The sign at path A is false.

Which path is the correct one?

	sign A	sign B	sign C
If path A			
If path B			
If path C			

Solution on page 478

P6-8 The Eighth Decision

He has made seven correct decisions in a row and is finding it difficult to focus on his golf swing. However, he must face his next challenge, and it comes after a double bogey on the eighth hole. The golfer's score-card tells him that one false sign points the way to the ninth tee, but the other two signs lead to open desert. He reads them as follows:

A
Either path B or C, or both, lead to the open desert.

B
This is not the path to take.

C
Either path A or B, or both, lead to the open desert.

Which path is correct?

	sign A	sign B	sign C
If path A			
If path B			
If path C			

Solution on page 479

P6-9 The Ninth Decision

The golfer finishes the ninth hole with another double bogey. It is a long way back to the clubhouse, and it is getting late. He quickly moves to the paths that await him. His scorecard indicates that at least two signs are false. He reads them carefully, below:

A
This is the correct way to the clubhouse.

B
At least one of signs A and C is true.

C
This is not the correct path to the clubhouse.

It has been dark for several hours and the golfer hasn't returned to the clubhouse. He apparently took the wrong path. Which one should he have taken?

	sign A	sign B	sign C
If path A			
If path B			
If path C			

Solution on page 480

7.
Namesakes

These puzzles involve the names of people and of other things. Your challenge is to correctly connect people's names with other names: who's named for what, and what's named for whom.

P7-1 Four Fishing Boats

Four close friends who are avid fishermen as well as horse owners have each named his fishing boat after the horse owned by one of the others. No two boats have the same name.

From the statements that follow, what is the name of each horse (one is Spike) and what name is given to each boat?

1. Jake's fishing boat is named after Jay's horse.
2. Jeb's horse is named King.
3. Joe's fishing boat is named Ace.
4. Jeb's fishing boat is not named Beau.

	horse	boat
Jake		
Jay		
Jeb		
Joe		

Solution on pages 481–482

P7-2 Knowheyan Paddle-bird Tournament

Knowhey is a planet in another galaxy on which a favorite game of the inhabitants is played with two or four players and involves hitting a feathered ball back and forth over a net using paddles. The inhabitants are very adept at this game and enjoy playing with visitors from other planets. An informal tournament is being played in which four teams are participating; each is comprised of one visitor and one inhabitant. Because the inhabitants' names are difficult to pronounce, to be congenial each Knowheyan player has adopted the name of one of the visitors, although no inhabitant is the namesake of the visitor with which he is teamed and no two teams contain the same pair of names.

From the following statements, determine which visitor is teamed with which inhabitant.

1. The visitor Larry is teamed with the inhabitant who is the namesake of the visitor who is teamed with the inhabitant using the name Lenny.

2. The visitor Lenny is teamed with the inhabitant who is the namesake of the visitor who is teamed with the inhabitant Larry.
3. The visitor Logan is teamed with the inhabitant who is the namesake of the visitor who is teamed with the inhabitant Lewis.
4. The inhabitant Lenny and his teammate won their game with the visitor Logan and his teammate.

Knoweyans

	Larry	Lenny	Logan	Lewis
Larry				
Lenny				
Logan				
Lewis				

visitors

Solution on pages 482–483

P7-3 Burglaries in the Neighborhood

There has been a series of neighborhood burglaries and six neighbors have acquired six dogs, ostensibly to serve as watchdogs. For some reason, the six neighbors each named his dog after one of the other neighbors, yet no two dogs were named after the same neighbor. (One of the six neighbors, it turns out, is the burglar.)

Based on the statements below, which neighbor owns which dog, and who is the burglar?

1. The dog named Moriarity is owned by the owner whose namesake is owned by Milton.
2. The dog named Marion is owned by the owner whose namesake is owned by Melville.
3. Milton's dog is not named Maurice or Martin.
4. The dog named Martin is owned by the owner whose namesake is owned by the owner whose namesake is owned by the burglar.
5. The dog named Melville is owned by the owner whose namesake is owned by Martin.

6. Milton's dog is the namesake of the owner of the dog whose namesake is the owner of the dog named Marion.

dogs

	Marion	Martin	Maurice	Melville	Milton	Moriarty
Marion						
Martin						
Maurice						
Melville						
Milton						
Moriarty						

owners

Solution on pages 483–484

P7-4 Wine Connoisseurs

Six couples who are wine enthusiasts belong to a wine-tasting club. At a recent holiday occasion they exchanged bottles of wine. Each couple gave a bottle of their favorite wine to one of the other couples.

Each couple is the namesake of one of the wines given, although no couple gave a wine of which they are a namesake, and no couple received a wine of which they are a namesake.

Which couples gave which wines and which wines did they receive?

1. The Sherrys received merlot from the namesakes of the wine given by the Chardonnays.
2. The namesakes of the wine received by the Chardonnays gave chardonnay and received burgundy.
3. The Merlots did not give or receive burgundy or bordeaux.
4. The port was received by the namesakes of the wine that was given to the Merlots.
5. The namesakes of the wine received by the Ports gave port and received wine that was the namesake of the couple that gave merlot.
6. The bordeaux was given by the couple that were the namesakes of the wine that was given by the

Ports, and was received by the namesakes of the
wine that was received by the Ports.

wines

	bord.	burg.	chard.	merlot	port	sherry
Bord.						
Burg.						
Chard.						
Merlot						
Port						
Sherry						

couples

Solution on pages 484–485

8.
Things in Order

These puzzles involve putting things (and people) in order. The reasoning process in solving the following puzzles is unlike the other puzzles in the book. No diagrams are needed, nor are any assumptions or considerations of veracity required. The challenge is to take the items listed and arrange them in the proper order, as described.

To solve these puzzles, list the items generally in the order described. Then carefully review the information given, and adjust the order of the items listed until it is completely consistent with the information provided. For most puzzles, this will require several realignments.

P8-1 Wood-Chopping Contest

In late autumn, the denizens known as the Forest People held their annual wood-chopping contest to provide fuel to last through the winter. Each participant was then ranked according to the amount of wood chopped. In this particular season, twelve of these forest denizens competed. From the following information, list the twelve participants in order, according to the amount of wood each chopped.

Evum chopped more wood than Estum, Edum, Eskum, and Ensum, and less than Egum, Elfum, Efrum, and Ekum. Ekum chopped less than Epum, and more than Esum, Eskum, and Ebum. Egum chopped more wood than Epum, who chopped more than Elfum, Estum, and Evum.

Eskum chopped more than Ensum, who chopped less than Esum, Evum, and Ebum. Ebum chopped less than Estum and Edum. Edum chopped less than Esum. Elfum chopped more than Efrum, who chopped more than Ekum and Evum. Evum chopped more than Esum, who chopped less than Estum, who chopped more than Ebum, who chopped more than Eskum and less than Edum.

Solution on page 486

P8-2 Goblins, Ogres, and Giants

From his home, which was well concealed from passersby, Elfum could observe which individuals were using a trail into the forest. During one period he counted fifteen goblins, ogres, and giants who passed his observation point. Considering that every third one was an ogre, and that numbers eight and fourteen were giants, which of the fifteen were goblins, which were ogres, and which were giants?

Hab came after Rio and Par, and before Tose. Coj came after Dino and Boe, who came after Geb, who was before Fane. Ocho came before Veb and Par, who came before Rio, who came after Ejo, who came after Par, who came after Veb. Deg came after Hab and before Tose, who came before Bib. Geb came after Zed, who came after Bib and before Fane, who came before Boe, who came before Dino.

Solution on pages 486–487

P8-3 Trees in the Forest

Many different varieties of tree grew in the forest inhabited by the Forest People. Walking along a small path, Ekum counted eighteen varieties of tree. Based on the statements that follow, in what order were the different varieties of tree aligned on each side of the path. ("Before and after" refers to the same side of the path? "Across from" means directly opposite, on the other side of the path.)

A cedar, which was after a birch, was before an elm, a fir, and an oak, which was across from a poplar, which was after an ash, a yew, and an aspen. A hickory was across from a maple, which was after the oak and the elm, which was after a willow. A pine was before the birch, which was after a hemlock, which was before the fir and across from an alder, which was after the aspen and before a juniper and a spruce, which was before the yew. A tamarack was before the poplar, which was before the hickory. The juniper was before the spruce, which was before the tamarack, which was before the ash and after the yew. The fir was before the willow and across from the yew.

Solution on page 487

P8-4 Fishing Flies

Henry Hackle is the proprietor of the Midville Fly-Fishing Shop. Part of his job is answering inquiries from his customers. Henry has been asked what his favorite fishing flies are and how he rates them, one to another. He has managed to narrow the list to sixteen, but has difficulty rating them in order of preference. The best he can do is compare each favorite fly to a few others.

You can help out by listing all of his favorite flies in the order in which they are favored, based on the information below:

The Gold Ribbed Hare's Ear is favored ahead of the Woolly Bugger, the Grey Wulff, and the Zug Bug, but behind the Olive Blue Dun and the Adams. The Royal Wulff, the Wright's Royal, and the Royal Humpy are favored ahead of the Light Cahill, the Elk Hair Caddis, and the Brook's Stone Fly, but behind the Maribou Muddler, which is favored ahead of the Grey Wulff and the Prince Nymph. Murphy's No. 1 is favored ahead of the Adams, the Elk Hair Caddis, the Gold Ribbed Hare's Ear, and the Woolly Bugger, which is favored ahead of the Maribou Muddler and the Joe's Hopper, which is rated behind the Zug Bug.

The Grey Wulff is favored ahead of the Elk Hair

Caddis, the Royal Humpy, and the Light Cahill, but behind the Royal Wulff, the Olive Blue Dun, and the Adams. The Royal Wulff is favored behind the Woolly Bugger and Murphy's No. 1, but ahead of the Wright's Royal, which is less favored than the Royal Humpy. The Prince Nymph is favored ahead of the Zug Bug and the Brook's Stone Fly, which is favored ahead of the Zug Bug.

The Olive Blue Dun is favored ahead of the Maribou Muddler and the Gold Ribbed Hare's Ear, but behind the Adams. The Elk Hair Caddis is favored behind the Wright's Royal and the Maribou Muddler, but ahead of the Light Cahill, which is favored ahead of the Joe's Hopper and the Prince Nymph.

Solution on page 488

P8-5 Varieties of Fruit

The ideal climate in the land of Hyperborea provided for the availability of a wide variety of fruit. At the fresh fruit stand in one village market, twenty varieties could be found arranged in two rows. Based on the information below, list the varieties of fruit in their proper order. ("To the right of" and "to the left of" means in the same row; "in front of" or "behind" means directly opposite in the adjacent row.)

The grapes were to the right of the lemons and the mangos, which were to the left of the nectarines, which were in front of the papayas. The cherries, which were behind the strawberries and to the right of the plums, were to the left of the persimmons, which were to the right of the loquats, which were to the left of the apricots. The oranges were to the right of the pears and to the left of the plums, which were to the right of the peaches, which were to the left of the cherries and to the right of the oranges.

The limes, which were in front of the pears, were to the left of the watermelons and the bananas, which were to the left of the blackberries, which were to the right of the watermelons, which were to the left of the strawberries and the bananas. The raspberries were to the left of the lemons, which were to the right of the blackberries and the strawberries, which were to the right of the bananas and to the left of the raspberries and the mangos, which were to the right of the lemons.

The nectarines were to the left of the grapes, which were to the right of the raspberries, which were to the right of the strawberries. The papayas were to the left of the guavas, which were to the right of the loquats, which were to the right of the cherries and to the left of the persimmons, which were to the left of the apricots.

Solution on page 488

P8-6 Chivalrous Knights

In the time of Sir Hector, knights were honored for their noble acts of chivalry, and they were rated accordingly. Eighteen knights and comparative ratings among them are indicated below. From this information, list them in the correct order in which they were rated.

Sir Hector, who was rated lower than Sir Resourceful, was rated higher that Sir Loyal and Sir Admirable, who was rated lower than Sir Dauntless and higher than Sir Virtue. Sir Intrepid was rated higher than Sir Gallant and Sir Fearless, who was rated lower than Sir Daring, who was rated lower than Sir Gallant. Sir Trustworthy was rated lower than Sir Resolute, who was rated higher than Sir Resourceful and Sir Bold.

Sir Victor was rated higher than Sir Virtue, who was rated higher than Sir True and Sir Dependable, who was rated lower than Sir True. Sir Bold was rated lower than Sir Trustworthy, who was rated higher than Sir Resourceful, who was rated lower than Sir Bold.

Sir Valorous was rated higher than Sir Gallant, and lower than Sir Intrepid. Sir Fearless was rated higher than Sir Faithful, who was rated higher than Sir Resolute. Sir Loyal, who was rated lower than Sir Dauntless, was rated higher than Sir Victor, who was rated higher than Sir Admirable.

Solution on page 489

P8-7 The Tournament Pavilions

On the occasion of a major festival and tournament, twenty renowned knights camped in two rows facing each other along one side of the field of competition. From the information below, determine the relative location of each knight's tent. ("To the right of" or "left of" means in the same row; "across from" means in the other row and directly opposite.)

Sir Fearless's tent was at an end of a row and across from Sir Daring's tent, which was in the easterly of the two rows. Sir Hector's tent was to the left of the tents of Sir Faithful, Sir Resolute, and Sir Dependable, whose tent was to the right of Sir Able's, Sir True's, and Sir Dauntless's tents.

The tent of Sir Victor was to the right of the tents of Sir Virtue and Sir Gallant, whose tent was across from that of Sir Faithful and of Sir Resourceful, whose tent was across from that of Sir Resolute.

The tent of Sir Trustworthy was to the right of the tent of Sir Dependable and across from the tent of Sir Intrepid, whose tent was to the left of that of Sir Resourceful. The tent of Sir Reliable was to the left of that of Sir Daring and to the right of the tents of Sir Victor, Sir Virtue, and Sir Gallant.

Sir Able's tent was to the right of the tent of Sir Resolute, whose tent was to the left of the tent of Sir Dependable, whose tent was to the right of that of Sir Loyal, whose tent was to the right of that of Sir Faithful. Sir Admirable's tent was to the left of that of Sir Gallant and to the right of that of Sir Valorous, whose tent was to the right of Sir Resourceful's, whose tent was to the right of Sir Bold's tent.

The tent of Sir Virtue was to the left of that of Sir Victor and to the right of that of Sir Gallant. Sir Hector's tent was to the left of that of Sir Faithful and to the right of the tent of Sir True, whose tent was to the right of that of Sir Dauntless.

Solution on pages 489–490

P8-8 Banners of the Winners

The banners of previous winners of the annual chariot races in Hyperborea are prominently displayed at the entrance to the sports stadium. Each of the sixteen banners is made up of two colors. From the information below, can you determine the placement of each banner on the display? ("To the right of" or "left of" means in the same row; "above" or "below" means in the same column.)

The burgundy and gray banner is below the red and emerald-green banner and above the gold on jade-green banner and the red on white banner, which is to the right of the sky-blue on silver banner and the cream on olive-green banner.

The sky-blue on silver banner is below the silver on black banner and to the left of the charcoal on orange banner and the black on white banner, which is to the right of the red on white banner, which is above the gold and jade-green banner. The gold on royal-blue banner is to the right of the gold on jade-green banner, the yellow on nut-brown banner, the bronze on cream banner, and the eggshell-blue and cream banner.

The forest-green on gold banner is to the left of the gold on jade-green banner, the yellow on nut-brown banner, and the copper on yellow banner, which is below the cream on olive banner, which is to the left of the sky-blue on silver banner, the red on white banner, and the black on white banner, which is above the eggshell-blue and cream banner, which is to the right of the gold on jade-green banner, which is to the right of the copper on yellow banner. The yellow on nut-brown banner is to the left of the gold on jade-green banner.

The olive on yellow banner is above the black on white banner, which is to the left of the charcoal on orange banner, which is above the bronze on cream banner, which is to the left of the gold on royal-blue banner, and to the right of the eggshell-blue and cream banner and the yellow on nut-brown banner, which is below the sky-blue on silver banner, which is to the left of the red on white banner.

Solution on page 490

P8-9 New Neighbors

Twenty-four families have recently moved into town on one new street. From the information presented below, can you determine the relative location of the home of each family on the street? ("To the right" or "left of" means on the same side of the street. "Across from" means on the other side of the street and directly opposite, facing into the street.)

The Maloneys live to the left of the Mayers, the Mayfields, and the Marlows, and across from the Mahoneys, who live on the east side of the street. The Mallettes live to the left of the Marlows, the Mastersons, and the Mallorys, who live to the right of the Malones, the Maxwells, and the Mayers. The Matlocks live to the right of the Mayfields, who live to the right of the Marshes and the Mallorys.

The Mathesons live to the right of the Marleaus, the Martins, and the Marquardts, who live to the right of the Macklins and the Matsens.

The Marshalls live to the left of the Mahoneys and to the right of the Mathesons, the Marleaus, and the Martins. The Mathews live to the left of the Majors and the Marquardts, and to the right of the Matsens, who live to the right of the Macklins.

The Malones live to the left of the Mastersons, who live to the left of the Mallorys, and to the right of the Mayburys, who live to the left of the Malones and to the right of the Marlows. The Majors live to the left of the Martins and to the right of the Magnans, who live to the right of the Marquardts, who live to the right of the Marsdens.

The Marleaus live to the left of the Mathesons and to the right of the Martins. The Mallettes live to the left of the Marlows and to the right of the Maxwells, who live to the right of the Mayers. The Marshes live to the right of the Mallorys.

Solution on page 491

P8-10 Devoted to Opera

Ms. Aria, an opera devotee, has attended in recent years a significant number of different operas at least once. Attempting to remember the order in which they were attended, she is only partially successful.

The lefthand column below lists those operas she recalls attending. To the right of each are the names of operas she can recall attending *before* that opera.

With this information, reconstruct the total list of operas in the order attended.

Opera attended	Operas attended previously
Rigoletto	Die Meistersinger, Carmen, Falstaff, Arabella
Aïda	Manon, Pagliacci, Don Pasquale, Lohengrin, Falstaff, Don Giovanni
Pagliacci	Don Pasquale, Manon, Cosí Fan Tutte, Lohengrin
La Bohême	La Gioconda, Don Carlos, Parsifal, Tristan and Isolde
Faust	Arabella, Parsifal, Otello, La Traviata

Madame Butterfly	La Bohême, Die Fledermaus, Tristan and Isolde, Cosí Fan Tutte, Don Pasquale, Aïda
Cosí Fan Tutte	Carmen, Die Meistersinger, Parsifal
La Traviata	Rigoletto
Boris Godunov	Tosca, Aïda, Cavalleria Rusticana, Carmen
Die Fledermaus	Cavalleria Rusticana, Peter Grimes, Don Pasquale, Don Carlos
Arabella	Elektra
Tristan and Isolde	Otello, The Bartered Bride, Manon, Rigoletto, Amahl and the Night Visitors, Faust
Die Meistersinger	Carmen, Tannhauser
Don Pasquale	Cavalleria Rusticana, Tannhauser, Tristan and Isolde
La Gioconda	Boris Godunov, Aïda, Otello, Cavalleria Rusticana
Falstaff	Don Giovanni, Arabella

Cavalleria Rusticana	Lohengrin
Tosca	Don Carlos
Elektra	Cosí Fan Tutte
Peter Grimes	Tosca, La Bohême, Don Carlos
Carmen	Don Giovanni, Tannhauser
Otello	The Bartered Bride, Tannhauser, Arabella, La Traviata
Don Carlos	Aïda, Don Pasquale
Tannhauser	Manon
Don Giovanni	Manon, Tannhauser
Lohengrin	Tristan and Isolde, Faust, Amahl and the Night Visitors, Don Giovanni
The Bartered Bride	Rigoletto, Amahl and the Night Visitors, Falstaff, Elektra, La Traviata
Parsifal	Die Meistersinger, Carmen, Manon, Don Giovanni
Amahl and the Night Visitors	Arabella, Cosí Fan Tutte, La Traviata, Elektra

Solution on page 492

9.
The Dragons
of Lidd

The greatest challenge and honor for a knight in the Kingdom of Lidd is to confront and slay a dragon. As a result, the dragon population in Lidd has been considerably reduced. Those dragons that have agreed to live peaceably have been put on the endangered species list and, by the king's decree, are protected.

Dragons in the Kingdom of Lidd are of two types. Some have reasoned accurately that devouring farm animals and their owners has attracted the attention of knights and is, in the long run, not a healthy thing for dragons to do. They have since totally refrained from this practice. These dragons are known as rationals, and they are the protected dragons.

Some dragons, on the other hand, have not learned

to fear humans and continue in their traditional ways. These dragons are known as predators, and they are not protected from confrontations with knights.

In addition to being rationals or predators, dragons in Lidd are of two different colors, related to their veracity. Gray rational dragons always speak the truth; red rational dragons always lie. Red predator dragons always speak the truth; gray predator dragons always lie.

It is necessary for knights to know which dragons are rationals and which dragons are predators. To tell if a dragon is protected, it would help to know its color. However, there is an affliction endemic to all humans in Lidd: they are colorblind. To each knight, all dragons look gray. Therefore, it is important to ask a dragon his type and color, and to attempt to determine whether the answers are truthful or false.

Your challenge is to determine the color and type of each dragon encountered in the following puzzles.

P9-1 Two Dragons

A knight approaches two dragons and inquires as to the color and type of each. Gray rationals and red predators always tell the truth; red rationals and gray predators always lie. The dragons respond below:

A. 1. I am gray.
   2. B is a predator.

B. 1. A is a predator.
   2. I am a rational.

	A	B
color		
type		

Solution on page 493

P9-2 Two More Dragons

Two knights in full armor approach two dragons and ask their types and colors. Gray rationals and red predators always speak the truth; red rationals and gray predators always lie. Their answers follow:

A. 1. B and I are rationals.
   2. Everything B says is false.

B. 1. A and I are both predators.
   2. I am red.

	A	B
color		
type		

Solution on page 494

P9-3 Three to One

A lone knight cautiously approaches three dragons and inquires as to their types and colors. Gray rationals and red predators always speak the truth; red rationals and gray predators always lie. They respond as follows:

A. 1. I am not a predator.
   2. B is gray.

B. 1. I am not a predator.
   2. C is gray.
   3. A's statements are true.

C. 1. All three of us are protected by the king's decree.
   2. A is red.
   3. B is red.

	A	B	C
color			
type			

Solution on pages 494–495

P9-4 Three to One Again

A knight alone warily approaches three dragons and politely asks the type and color of each. Gray rationals and red predators always speak the truth; red rationals and gray predators always lie. Their answers are below:

A. 1. I am a rational, but I intend to eat you anyway.
   2. Neither B nor C is a rational.

B. 1. A is a rational that has spoken falsely.
   2. I am a rational.

C. 1. A and B are both predators.
   2. I am a gray rational.
   3. A's second statement is false.

	A	B	C
color			
type			

Solution on pages 495–496

P9-5 Whose Colors Are the Same?

Two knights encounter three dragons and ask each his color and type. Gray rationals and red predators always speak the truth; red rationals and gray predators always lie. They respond below:

A. 1. I am a rational.
    2. Dragon C and I are not the same color.

B. 1. Dragon A is a rational.
    2. I am not red.

C. 1. Dragon B is a predator.
    2. Dragon A and I are the same color.

	A	B	C
color			
type			

Solution on pages 496–497

P9-6 Three on Three

Three knights looking for adventure approach three dragons and ask for their colors and types. Gray rationals and red predators always speak the truth; red rationals and gray predators always lie. The three dragons answer below:

A. 1. B and C are predators.
   2. I am a rational.

B. 1. Both A and C speak the truth.
   2. I am not the same type as A.

C. 1. I am not the same type as A.
   2. A and B are both gray.

	A	B	C
color			
type			

Solution on page 497

P9-7 Are There Any Predators Left?

Two knights looking for some action approach three dragons. They inquire as to each dragon's type and color. Gray rationals and red predators always speak the truth; red rationals and gray predators always lie. The three dragons respond as follows:

A. 1. Ask B what my type is; he will give you a truthful answer.
   2. C is red.

B. 1. A and I are both rationals.
   2. C is a predator.

C. 1. A and B are both predators.
   2. B is gray.

	A	B	C
color			
type			

Solution on page 498

P9-8 How Many Are Rationals?

A lone knight happens on three large dragons and asks their colors and types. Gray rationals and red predators always speak the truth; red rationals and gray predators always lie. The three dragons respond below:

A. 1. Neither B nor I is gray.
   2. C claims to be red.
   3. Only two of the three of us speak the truth.

B. 1. I am a rational.
   2. A claims to be a predator.
   3. A's third statement is false.

C. 1. B is a predator.
   2. A claims to be a rational.

	A	B	C
color			
type			

Solution on pages 498–499

P9-9 Three on Three Again

Three knights seeking action confront three dragons and ask the type and color of each. Gray rationals and red predators always speak the truth; red rationals and grey predators always. The dragons' answers follow:

A. 1. I am neither a red rational nor a gray predator.
   2. C's statements are true.

B. 1. A is either a red rational or a gray predator.
   2. C would agree with me about A.

C. 1. There is only one rational among the three of us, and it is I.
   2. A is a red predator.

	A	B	C
color			
type			

Solution on pages 499–500

P9-10 Four Dragons

Two knights cautiously approach four dragons and ask each about his color and type. Gray rationals and red predators always speak the truth; red rationals and gray predators always lie. The four dragons respond:

A. 1. Only two of the four of us speak the truth.
   2. I am not a predator.
   3. C always lies.

B. 1. Both A and I speak the truth.
   2. D and I are the same color.

C. 1. I am the only one among us that speaks the truth.
   2. I am not a predator.

D. 1. A does not speak the truth.
   2. C and I are the same color.

	A	B	C	D
color				
type				

Solution on pages 500–501

The Dragons
from Wonk

Dragons from the adjacent Land of Wonk are either
rationals or predators. However, they are all blue and
they all lie. It is not unusual for knights to encounter
blue dragons that have crossed into the Kingdom of
Lidd.

P9-11 One Is Blue

Two knights looking for a confrontation encounter two dragons, one of which is blue, and ask their types and colors. Gray rationals and red predators always speak the truth; red rationals and gray predators always lie; blue rationals and blue predators always lie. The two dragons answer as follows:

A. 1. B is a predator.
   2. I am a rational.

B. 1. I am either a red rational or a gray predator.
   2. A is a predator.

	A	B
color		
type		

Solution on page 501

P9-12 Two of Three Are Blue

Three dragons, two of which are blue, are approached by three knights, who inquire as to their types and colors. Gray rationals and red predators always speak the truth; red rationals and gray predators always lie; blue rationals and blue predators always lie. Their responses follow:

A. 1. I am a rational.

B. 1. I am not gray.
   2. A and C are not the same type.

C. 1. I am a predator.

	A	B	C
color			
type			

Solution on page 502

P9-13 One of Three Is Blue

This time, a lone knight confronts three dragons, one of which is blue. The knight asks their types and colors. As is known, gray rationals and red predators always speak the truth; red rationals and gray predators always lie; blue rationals and blue predators always lie. The three dragons reply as follows:

A. 1. B is blue.
    2. I am the only rational among the three of us.

B. 1. C is blue.
    2. C is a rational.

C. 1. A's first statement is false.
    2. I am the blue dragon.

	A	B	C
color			
type			

Solution on pages 502–503

P9-14 At Least One Is a Blue Dragon

A group of four knights traveling together encounters four dragons, at least one of which is blue. The dragons are asked their types and colors. Gray rationals and red predators always speak the truth; red rationals and gray predators always lie; blue rationals and blue predators always lie.

A. 1. I am not a blue dragon.
   2. If asked, C would state that D is a predator.
   3. Only one of us is a blue dragon.

B. 1. C is a predator.
   2. I am a blue dragon.

C. 1. I am a predator.
   2. A is not a blue dragon.
   3. Three of us are rationals.

D. 1. B is not a blue dragon.
   2. If asked, B would state that A is a predator.

	A	B	C	D
color				
type				

Solution on pages 503–504

P9-15 How Many Blue Dragons?

A lone knight rounds a bend in the trail and finds himself facing four large dragons. He inquires as to their types and colors. Gray rationals and red predators always speak the truth; red rationals and gray predators always lie; blue rationals and blue predators always lie. Their answers follow:

A. 1. If you want to know my type, C will give you a true answer.
   2. D is blue.

B. 1. A and I are both rationals.
   2. Three of us are blue.

C. 1. If you want to know A's type, B will give you a true answer.
   2. Only one of us is blue.
   3. D's statements are false.

D. 1. Three of us are predators.
   2. A is a rational.
   3. A is not blue.

	A	B	C	D
color				
type				

Solution on pages 504–505

SOLUTIONS

1. Hypotheses

The Voyage of Singood the Sailor

S1-1 A Giant Fish

CONSIDERATIONS

From statement 1, if the fish had just consumed a ship and several whales, it was evening. From statement 3, if it was evening, the giant fish was too old and slow. Therefore, statement 1 is not valid: the giant fish had not just consumed a ship and several whales.

From statement 4, if the giant fish was too old, it was morning. From statement 2, if it was morning, the ship and crew were too small to be noticed. Therefore, statement 4 is not valid: the giant fish was not too old and slow.

Therefore, the solution must be that it was morning and the ship and crew were too small to be noticed by the giant fish.

SUMMARY SOLUTION

It was morning and the ship and crew were too small to be noticed by the giant fish.

S1-2 An Enchanted Island

CONSIDERATIONS

From statement 3, if A was the first mate, B was the second mate. However, from statement 2, if B was not Singood, C was the first mate. Therefore, we can conclude that A was not the first mate and, from statement 2, B was not the first mate. Therefore, C was the first mate.

From statement 1, since B was not the first mate, A was not Singood. Therefore, A was the second mate and B was Singood. (Note: Even though the assumption in statement 2 is invalid [B was Singood], this does not preclude C's being the first mate.)

SUMMARY SOLUTION

A was the second mate
B was Singood
C was the first mate

S1-3 A Third Island

CONSIDERATIONS

From statement 1, if the palms vanished first, the fruit trees were third. However, from statement 2, if the fruit trees were third to vanish, the waterfall was first. Therefore, the palms did not vanish first.

From statement 3, if the waterfall vanished first, the clear lake vanished fourth. However, from statement 4, if the clear lake was fourth, the fruit trees were first. Therefore, the waterfall was not first.

From statement 5, since neither the waterfall nor the wavy palms vanished first, the clear lake vanished first.

From statement 6, since the clear lake vanished first, the fruit trees and waterfall must have vanished second and third in some order, and the wavy palms vanished fourth.

From statement 7, since the wavy palms vanished fourth, the waterfall vanished third and the fruit trees vanished second.

SUMMARY SOLUTION

clear lake	1st
fruit trees	2nd
waterfall	3rd
wavy palms	4th

S1-4 Return to the Ship

CONSIDERATIONS

From statement 1, we can conclude that Singood was either first or third to take a turn rowing.

From statement 2, if the first mate was first to take a turn rowing, the second mate was second to take a turn. However, from statement 3, if the second mate was second to take a turn, the first mate was third in the rotation. Therefore, the assumption in statement 2, that the first mate was first to take a turn, is not valid. The first mate was either second or third in the rotation.

From statement 4, for the first mate to be third to take a turn, Singood must be second to take a turn. However, from statement 1, we know that Singood was either first or third to take a turn. Therefore, the first mate was not third. Therefore, he was second to take a turn.

From statement 5, since the second mate was not second to take a turn, the assumption that he was not third is invalid. The second mate was third and Singood was first in the rotation.

Singood	1st
first mate	2nd
second mate	3rd

S1-5 A Gigantic Bird

CONSIDERATIONS

From statements 3 and 2, statement 3 is invalid: the gigantic bird's wingspan was not 40 or 50 meters wide.

From statement 4, the gigantic bird's wingspan was 20 or 30 meters wide.

Therefore, from statement 1, it carried the three shipmates 50 leagues.

SUMMARY SOLUTION

Bird's wingspan was 20 or 30 meters wide; it carried shipmates 50 leagues.

S1-6 Attacked by a Giant Serpent

CONSIDERATIONS

From statement 1, if Singood was attacked by the serpent, the first mate stayed in the tree. If so, the second mate must have hurried to the rescue. From statement 2, if the first mate stayed in the tree, the second mate did not go to the rescue. Therefore, Singood was not attacked by the serpent.

From statement 3, if the second mate did not stay in the tree, the first mate was attacked by the serpent. Therefore, the second mate was not attacked by the serpent. Therefore, the first mate was attacked by the serpent.

From statement 4, if Singood stayed in the tree, the first mate went to the rescue. Therefore, Singood did not stay in the tree. Therefore, Singood went to the rescue, and the second mate stayed in the tree.

SUMMARY SOLUTION

Singood	went to rescue
first mate	attacked by serpent
second mate	stayed in tree

S1-7 Captured by the One-Eyed Giant

CONSIDERATIONS

If statement 1 is valid, then Singood's idea was to stab the giant in his one eye, the second mate's idea was to climb over the sleeping giant, and the first mate's idea was to hide under the bones. From statement 2, if the first mate's idea was to stab the giant in the eye or hide under the bones, then Singood's idea was to climb over the giant. Therefore, we can conclude that statement 1 is not valid: Singood's idea was not to stab the giant in the eye.

From statement 3, if Singood's idea was either of the other two options, then the first mate's idea was to stab the giant in the eye. Therefore, the first mate's idea was to stab the giant. From statement 2, Singood's idea was to climb over the sleeping giant, and the second mate's idea was to hide under the pile of bones.

SUMMARY SOLUTION

Singood	climb over sleeping giant
first mate	stab giant in eye
second mate	hide under bones

S1-8 Escape from the Giant

CONSIDERATIONS

From statement 2, if the journey took three months the escape was by climbing over the sleeping giant. From statement 3, the journey took two months if the escape was by climbing over the sleeping giant. Therefore, the journey did not take three months. Therefore, it took two months.

Statement 3 is invalid, since the escape by climbing over the sleeping giant depended on the journey's taking two months. However, from statement 1, if the journey took two months, then the escape was by hiding beneath a pile of bones.

Statement 4 is valid; the escape was not by stabbing the giant in the eye, since the journey took two months.

Therefore, the escape was by hiding beneath a pile of bones until the giant left the cave, and the journey took two months.

SUMMARY SOLUTION

Escape made by hiding under bones; journey took two months.

S1-9 An Attack by Giant Spiders

CONSIDERATIONS

From statement 1, since either the spider with six useful legs or the spider with seven useful legs was injured by Singood, the spider with five legs was not injured by Singood.

From statement 2, since the spider with five useful legs was not injured by Singood, the spider with seven useful legs was not injured by the second mate.

From statement 3, since the spider with five useful legs was not injured by Singood, the spider with six useful legs was not injured by the first mate. Therefore, by statement 4, the spider with seven useful legs was injured by Singood.

Therefore, it's the spider with six useful legs that was injured by the second mate, and the spider with five useful legs was injured by the first mate.

SUMMARY SOLUTION

Singood	spider with 7 useful legs
first mate	spider with 5 useful legs
second mate	spider with 6 useful legs

S1-10 Serpentmares!

CONSIDERATIONS

From statement 3, if Singood was not devoured by either the black or blue serpent, the second mate was devoured by the red serpent. Therefore, Singood was not devoured by the red serpent.

From statement 1, if the second mate was not devoured by either the blue serpent or the green serpent, the first mate was devoured by the red serpent. Therefore, the second mate was not devoured by the red serpent. Therefore, the first mate was devoured by the red serpent.

Therefore, from statement 4, Singood was not devoured by the blue serpent. Therefore, since, from statement 3, the second mate was not devoured by the red serpent, Singood was devoured by the black serpent.

From statement 2, the second mate was devoured by the green serpent. The blue serpent went away hungry.

SUMMARY SOLUTION

Singood	black serpent
first mate	red serpent
second mate	green serpent

S1-11 Contest on the Beach

CONSIDERATIONS

From statement 1, if the first mate won the race down the beach, Singood won the coconut throw. If so, the second mate won the tree climb. However, from statement 3, if the second mate won the tree climb, the first mate won the coconut throw. Therefore, the first mate did not win the race down the beach.

From statement 5, if Singood won the race down the beach, the first mate won the tree climb. If so, the second mate won the coconut throw. However, from statement 2, if the second mate won the coconut throw, the first mate won the race down the beach. Therefore, Singood did not win the race down the beach. Therefore, the race was won by the second mate.

Therefore, from statement 4, Singood won the tree climb, and the first mate won the coconut throw.

SUMMARY SOLUTION

Singood	tree climb
first mate	coconut throw
second mate	race down the beach

S1-12 The Rescue

CONSIDERATIONS

From statement 1, if the rescue ship did not have four masts, then it was the white ship. From statement 5, if the rescue ship had three masts, it was not the white ship. Therefore, it was not the white ship.

From statement 2, if the black ship was the rescue ship, it had four masts. However, from statement 3, if the rescue ship had four masts, it was not black. Therefore, it was not black.

Therefore, from statement 4, the rescue ship was green and had four masts.

SUMMARY SOLUTION

The ship was green and had four masts.

Sir Hector Heroic
the Dragon Fighter

S1-13 A Contest

CONSIDERATIONS

From statements 1 and 5, Sir Able did not win the contest. From statements 2, 6, and 4, Sir Hector did not win. Since we know that both Sir Hector and Sir Gallant camped out overnight in the backcountry, then, from statement 3, Sir Gallant was not the winner.

By elimination, Sir Bold was the contest winner.

SUMMARY SOLUTION

Sir Bold was the contest winner.

S1-14 Seeking Adventure

CONSIDERATIONS

From statement 3, Sir Bold either confronted a sorcerer or battled a giant. From statement 2, either Sir Hector or Sir Able battled a giant. Therefore, Sir Bold did not battle a giant; he confronted a sorcerer.

From statement 1, if Sir Gallant did not confront a sorcerer, Sir Hector battled a dragon. Therefore, Sir Hector battled a dragon. Therefore, Sir Able battled a giant, and Sir Gallant battled a dragon.

SUMMARY SOLUTION

Sir Able battled a giant.
Sir Bold confronted a sorcerer.
Sir Gallant battled a dragon.
Sir Hector battled a dragon.

S1-15 The Sword-Fighting Matches

CONSIDERATIONS

From statement 1, if Sir Hector lost, sir Able won. If so, Sir Bold also won. However, from statement 3, if Sir Bold won, Sir Hector must have also won. Therefore, Sir Hector did not lose. Therefore, from statement 2, since Sir Hector won his match, Sir Bold was the knight who lost.

SUMMARY SOLUTION
Sir Bold was the knight who lost.

S1-16 Murder in the Black Castle

CONSIDERATIONS

From statement 1, if the knight in room 1 was the culprit, the knight in room 3 was the victim. However, from statement 3, if the knight in room 3 was the victim, the knight in room 2 was the culprit. Therefore, the knight in room 1 was not the culprit. From statement 7, if the knight in room 2 was the culprit, the servant was the victim. However, from statement 5, it is clear that the servant was not the victim. Therefore, the knight in room 2 was not the culprit.

From statement 6, if the knight in room 3 was the culprit, the knight in room 2 was the victim. However, from statement 2, if the knight in room 2 was the victim, the servant was the culprit. Therefore, the knight in room 3 was not the culprit. From statement 4, if the servant was the culprit, the knight in room 3 was the victim. However, from statement 3, we know that if the knight in room 3 was the victim, the knight in room 2 was the culprit. Therefore, the servant was not the culprit. Therefore, the remaining suspect, the master, must be the culprit, and the knight in room 1, the only knight not accounted for, was the victim.

SUMMARY SOLUTION

The master was the culprit; the knight in room 1 was the victim.

S1-17 The Mysterious Masked Miscreant

CONSIDERATIONS

From statement 1, if Sir Hector was overwhelmed by the miscreant's evil face, it was morning. However, from statement 3, if it was morning, Sir Hector had forgotten his sword. Therefore, Sir Hector was not overwhelmed by the evil face. From statement 2, if Sir Hector's fellow knights saved him, it was early afternoon, which is inconsistent with statement 4. Therefore, the confrontation did not take place in the early afternoon, and Sir Hector's fellow knights did not arrive to save him. From statement 4, if it was early evening, then Sir Hector's fellow knights arrived just in time to save him. But this is inconsistent with statement 2. So it was not early evening. Therefore, from statement 3, it was morning and Sir Hector had forgotten his sword, so did not stay to do battle.

SUMMARY SOLUTION

It was morning; Sir Hector had forgotten his sword, so did not stay to do battle.

S1-18 Who Saw Which Giant?

CONSIDERATIONS

From statement 2, if the assumption that Sir Able was not accurate in what he observed was valid, giant number two is guilty. From statement 1, if giant number one were guilty, Sir Hector was accurate in what he observed. From statement 4, if Sir Hector's description was accurate, so was Sir Bold's. However, from statement 3, it would validate the assumption in statement 2. In either case, giant number two is guilty. (Note: If Sir Hector's description were accurate, this would not necessarily preclude the assumption in statement 1 from being invalid.)

SUMMARY SOLUTION

Giant number two is guilty.

S1-19 Sir Hector's Most Challenging Adventure

CONSIDERATIONS

From statement 1, neither Grimsby nor the miscreant was the most challenging unless the dragon was not the second most challenging.

From statement 2, if the confrontation with the dragon was the second most challenging, neither the rescue from the black tower nor the sorcerer was the most challenging. Therefore, the confrontation with the dragon was not the second most challenging (as this would eliminate all five adventures as most challenging), and (from statement 1) either the encounter with Grimsby or the confrontation with the masked miscreant was the most challenging. The rescue from the black tower cannot be the most challenging. Therefore, from statement 4, the confrontation with the sorcerer cannot be the second most challenging.

From statement 3, if Grimsby the Giant was not the second most challenging, the masked miscreant was the most challenging. Therefore, the masked miscreant was the most challenging.

SUMMARY SOLUTION

The masked miscreant was the most challenging.

S1-20 Four Fair Damsels in Distress

CONSIDERATIONS

From statement 4, either Maid Matilda was rescued from the miscreant's hideout, or neither she nor Maid Morgana was. From statement 1, since Maid Morgana was not rescued from the miscreant's hideout, Maid Marie was rescued from a castle tower.

From statement 3, since Maid Marie was rescued from a castle tower, Maid Mary was rescued from two giants. Therefore, from statement 2, Maid Matilda was rescued from the miscreant's hideout. Therefore, Maid Morgana must have been rescued from a dragon's lair.

SUMMARY SOLUTION

Maid Marie	castle tower
Maid Mary	two giants
Maid Morgana	dragon's lair
Maid Matilda	miscreant's hideout

S1-21 Encounter with a Gigantic Serpentlike Creature

CONSIDERATIONS

From statement 1, if Sir Gallant did the fighting, Sir Hector observed. If so, Sir Resolute went home. However, from statement 5, if Sir Hector observed, Sir Resolute did the fighting. Therefore, Sir Gallant did not do the fighting.

From statement 2, if Sir Hector did the fighting, Sir Gallant went home. If so, Sir Resolute observed. However, from statement 4, if Sir Resolute observed, Sir Gallant did the fighting. Therefore, Sir Hector did not do the fighting. Therefore, Sir Resolute must have done the fighting.

From statement 3, if Sir Gallant went home, Sir Resolute observed. However, since we know that Sir Resolute did the fighting, Sir Gallant did not go home. Therefore, Sir Gallant observed, and Sir Hector went home.

SUMMARY SOLUTION

Sir Resolute   did fighting
Sir Gallant   observed
Sir Hector   went home

CONSIDERATIONS

Consider the assumption in statement 1 to be valid. If so, Sir Gallant was one of the two who confronted the giant. If the assumption is invalid, either Sir Hector or Sir Victor was one of the two who confronted the giant. Therefore, whether or not the assumption in statement 1 is valid or invalid, we can conclude that the pair who confronted the giant were not Sir Able and Sir Bold, Sir Able and Sir Resolute, or Sir Bold and Sir Resolute.

From statement 3, the two who confronted the giant were not Sir Bold and Sir Gallant, Sir Bold and Sir Victor, or Sir Gallant and Sir Victor.

From statement 4, the two who confronted the giant were not Sir Hector and Sir Gallant, Sir Hector and Sir Resolute, or Sir Gallant and Sir Resolute.

From statement 5, Sir Hector did not confront the giant, since we know that, from statement 4, he did not confront the giant along with either Sir Gallant or Sir Resolute.

From statement 6, Sir Victor must have been one of the two who confronted the giant, as the statement identifies three of the four knights not eliminated.

From statement 2, since Sir Victor was one of the

two who confronted the giant, the other, by elimination, must have been Sir Resolute.

SUMMARY SOLUTION
Sir Resolute and Sir Victor confronted the giant.

S1-23 Victory at the Grand Tournament

CONSIDERATIONS
From statement 1, if Sir Gallant was victorious, Sir Hector was not victorious. If so, Sir Able, Sir Bold, or Sir Resolute was also victorious. From statement 2, if Sir Able was victorious, Sir Gallant was not victorious; and from statement 4, if Sir Resolute was victorious, then Sir Able was victorious; and from statement 3, if Sir Hector was not victorious, neither was Sir Bold victorious. Therefore, Sir Gallant was not one of the two victorious knights.

From statement 5, if Sir Bold was victorious, Sir Able was not victorious. If so, Sir Gallant, Sir Hector, or Sir Resolute was also victorious. However, we know Sir Gallant was not victorious; and from statement 4, Sir Resolute's being victorious depends on Sir Able's being victorious; and from statement 6, Sir Hector's being victorious depends on Sir Resolute's being victorious. Therefore, Sir Bold was not one of the two victorious knights.

From statement 6, if Sir Hector was victorious, Sir Resolute was victorious. From statement 4, Sir Resolute's being victorious relies on Sir Able's being victorious. Therefore, Sir Hector was not victorious.

SUMMARY SOLUTION

The two victorious knights were Sir Able and Sir Resolute.

S1-24 Knights' Adversaries

CONSIDERATIONS

Consider statement 4: if Sir Gallant's skill was not dealing with dragons, then his skill was not dealing with giants, as the skill would belong to Sir Hector.

From statement 7, Sir Able could not be the most skilled at dealing with giants, as if Sir Gallant's skill was not dealing with dragons, then (from statement 4) Sir Hector's skill was dealing with giants.

From statement 6, as we know that Sir Able was not the most skilled at dealing with giants, Sir Hector's skill was not dealing with sorcerers. Therefore, from statement 2, Sir Bold's skill was not dealing with giants.

Therefore, Sir Hector was the most skilled at dealing with giants.

From statement 1, Sir Able was not the most skilled at dealing with dragons. From statement 3, since Sir Able's skill was not dealing with dragons, Sir Bold's skill was not dealing with sorcerers.

Therefore, Sir Able's skill was dealing with sorcerers. Sir Gallant and Sir Bold dealt, in some order, with giant serpents and dragons. But from statement 5, Sir Gallant could not have dealt with giant serpents. Therefore, Sir Gallant's skill was dealing with dragons, and Sir Bold dealt with giant serpents.

SUMMARY SOLUTION

Sir Able's skill	sorcerers
Sir Bold's skill	giant serpents
Sir Gallant's skill	dragons
Sir Hector's skill	giants

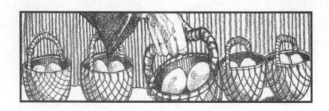

2. Who Dunnit?

S2-1 Supermarket Theft

CONSIDERATIONS

Consider that the guilty party's statement is true; the other two statements are false.

Assume that A is guilty. If so, A's statement must be true, making B guilty. Therefore, A is not the thief.

Assume B did it. However, since there is only one true statement, B's statement, that A's statement is true, makes two true statements. Therefore, B is innocent. Therefore, C's statement that A's statement is false is true. C is guilty.

SUMMARY SOLUTION

C is the thief.

S2-2 Bicycle Thefts

CONSIDERATIONS

Consider that the statement by the guilty party is false and the other statements are true.

Assume that B is guilty. If so, B's statement must be false, and A's statement must be true, making C guilty. Therefore, since only one is guilty, it is not B. Assume C is guilty. However, there is only one guilty suspect, and B and C are in agreement. Therefore, B and C both make true statements. A, whose statement is false, is guilty.

SUMMARY SOLUTION

A did it.

S2-3 Pool Party Push

CONSIDERATIONS

Consider that only one of the four suspects speaks truthfully.

Assume A's statement is false. If so, neither B nor C is guilty. Therefore, the guilty party is either A or D. Without more information, however, we cannot determine which one is guilty. Therefore, A's statement is the true one. Either B or C did it. B's statement must be false; C is guilty.

SUMMARY SOLUTION

C did it.

S2-4 The Impostor Surgeon

CONSIDERATIONS

Consider that the guilty party makes one true and one false statement.

Assume B is the impostor. If so, B's statements are both false. Therefore, B is not the impostor. Assume that C is the impostor. If so, both of C's statements are true. Therefore, C is not the impostor. Therefore, A is the impostor. His first statement is false and second statement is true.

SUMMARY SOLUTION

A did it.

S2-5 Granny Smith's Famous Pecan Pie

CONSIDERATIONS

Consider that only one suspect speaks the truth.

Assume that A is guilty. If so, his statement and B's are both true. Therefore, A is not guilty. Assume that B is guilty. If so, the statements by B and D are both true. Therefore, B didn't do it. Assume that C is guilty. If so, all four statements are false. Therefore, C is not guilty.

C's statement is the only true one; D is guilty.

SUMMARY SOLUTION

D is guilty.

S2-6 Two Scam Hustlers

CONSIDERATIONS

Consider that the two guilty ones make false statements; the others make true statements.

Assume that B is guilty. If so, from B's statement, C is also guilty. If so, from C's statement, D is also guilty. Therefore, since there are only two guilty parties, B is not guilty.

Therefore, from B's statement. C is not guilty; from C's statement, D is not guilty; from D's statement A is guilty; and from A's statement E is guilty.

SUMMARY SOLUTION

A and E are guilty.

S2-7 Who Stole the Goat?

CONSIDERATIONS

Consider that the quarterback and the center make two false statements; the running back makes one true and one false statement; and the defensive end makes two true statements.

Suspect D's first statement must be true. D is the running back, as he is the only one who can make that statement. Therefore, his second statement is false; the quarterback did not do it.

A's first statement is true. Therefore, he is the defensive end. The first statements of B and C are false: B is the quarterback and C is the center.

A's second statement is the only other true one; the center did it.

SUMMARY SOLUTION

A is the defensive end.
B is the quarterback.
C is the center.
D is the running back.

The center did it.

S2-8 What's the Crime?

CONSIDERATIONS

Consider that each suspect makes one true and two false statements.

A's third statement is true, so his other statements are false. Therefore, B is the guilty party.

Since we know that A is innocent, C's third statement is true, so his other statements are false. Therefore B's first statement is true.

B is guilty of robbing a service station.

SUMMARY SOLUTION

B robbed a service station.

S2-9 The Hood-Ornament Thefts

CONSIDERATIONS

Consider that only one of the guilty party's statements is true.

Assume that B is guilty. If so, both of B's statements are false. Therefore, B is not the culprit.

Assume that C is guilty. If so, both of C's statements are true. Therefore, C is not guilty.

Assume that D did it. If so, both of D's statements are false. Therefore, D is not guilty.

A did it. His first statement is false and second statement is true.

SUMMARY SOLUTION

A is guilty.

S2-10 Thanksgiving Dinner

CONSIDERATIONS

Consider that each of the suspects makes at least one false statement.

Assume A is the culprit. If so, A's and B's statements are true. Therefore, A is not guilty.

Assume that B is guilty. If so, again A's and B's statements are true. B did not do it.

C is the guilty party. All statements are false.

SUMMARY SOLUTION

C is the culprit.

S2-11 Car Thefts

CONSIDERATIONS

Consider that one suspect makes three true statements, and one makes three false statements. How the third suspect responds is unknown.

A's second statement must be false. Otherwise it would be a contradiction. Therefore, at least one of his statements is true. A is the suspect whose veracity is unknown.

B's second statement admits to an untruthful statement. B must be the suspect with three false statements, and C the suspect with all true statements. From B's first statement, which must be false, B is guilty.

SUMMARY SOLUTION

B did it.

S2-12 Residence Burglaries

CONSIDERATIONS

Consider that each suspect makes at least two false statements.

Assume that A is the burglar, as his second statement claims. If so, his third statement, that B's statement that C is the burglar is false, must be true. Therefore, since A would have at least two true statements, he is not guilty.

Assume that C is the burglar. If so, B's second statement is truthful, and B's third statement disputing A's third statement (that B's second statement is false) is also truthful. Therefore, C is not the burglar.

Therefore, B is the burglar. His first statement, that he doesn't know C, is false, as are his second and third statements. A's first and second statements are false, and C's first and third statements are false. B is guilty.

SUMMARY SOLUTION

B is the burglar.

S2-13 Who Murdered Quick-Hands Eddie?

CONSIDERATIONS

Consider that two of the three witnesses make no true statements. The truthfulness of the third witness is unknown.

Assume that A's claim that Rocky is guilty is true. If so, two of A's statements are true, none of B's statements are true, and one of C's statements is true. Therefore, Rocky did not do it.

Assume that C's claim that Phil the Enforcer is guilty is true. If so, one of A's statements is true, none of B's statements is true, and two of C's statements are true. Therefore, Phil the Enforcer did not do it.

Therefore, Harry the Hulk did it, as claimed by B. A makes no true statements, B makes two true statements, and C makes no true statements.

Harry the Hulk did it.

SUMMARY SOLUTION

Harry the Hulk is the culprit.

S2-14 Who Cheated at Poker?

CONSIDERATIONS

Consider that each player makes one true and one false statement.

First, assume that A is guilty. If so, both of A's statements are false. Therefore, A did not do it.

Assume that B is guilty. If so, both of B's statements are true. Therefore, B did not do it.

Now, assume that C is guilty. If so, both of C's statements are false. Therefore, C did not do it.

Assume that D did it. If so, both of D's statements are false. Therefore, D is innocent. Therefore, E did it. E's first statement is true and second statement is false.

SUMMARY SOLUTION

E is guilty.

S2-15 Which of the Three Is Innocent?

CONSIDERATIONS

Consider that the two culprits truthfully confess their crimes, but the innocent boy falsely confesses to one. Each boy makes one true and two false statements.

Assume that Junior is innocent. If so, Timmy's first statement must be his true statement, and his second and third statements are false. However, if Junior is innocent, Timmy's third statement is true. Therefore, Junior is not innocent.

Assume that Timmy is innocent. If so, all three of Junior's statements are true. Therefore, Timmy is not innocent.

Therefore, Sonny is innocent.

SUMMARY SOLUTION

Sonny did not do it.

S2-16 Who Put the Rattlesnake in Henry's Garage?

CONSIDERATIONS

Consider that all statements are true except any directly mentioning the culprit.

Assume that B is guilty. If so, B's first statement must be true. It claims that A's first statement, that C is not guilty, is false. Since there is only one guilty party, B is innocent.

Assume that C is guilty. If so, B's second statement confirms C's first statement. If C were guilty, B's second statement, which refers directly to C, would deny the truth of C's first statement. Therefore, C is not the guilty party.

Therefore, A is the culprit. B's first statement and C's second statement are both false.

SUMMARY SOLUTION
A did it.

S2-17 Theft of a Suit from Fred's Men's Fashions

CONSIDERATIONS

Consider that one suspect makes three true statements; one makes two true and one false statement; one makes one true and two false statements; and one makes three false statements.

Assume that A is the culprit. If so, A's first statement is true; B's first statement is true; C's first and second statements are true; and D's first statement is true. Therefore, since one of the suspects makes no true statements, A is innocent.

Assume that C is the culprit. If so, A's first statement is true; B's first statement is true; C's first statement is true; and D's second statement is true. Therefore, it is not C who is the thief.

Assume that D is guilty. If so, A's second statement is true; B's first statement is true; C's first statement is true; and D's second statement is true. Therefore, D is innocent.

Therefore, B is the thief, as indicated by D's second statement, which is false. A's first statement is true, B's first and third statements are true; C's three statements are true; and D's three statements are false.

SUMMARY SOLUTION
B is the thief.

S2-18 Stolen Golf Clubs

CONSIDERATIONS
Consider that no two suspects make the same number of true statements.

Assume that B is guilty. If so, B's first statement is true, and second and third statements are false. A's first statement is true, and second and third statements are false. C's second statement is true, and first and third statements are false. So B is not guilty.

Assume that C is guilty. If so, C's first and second statements are true and third statement is false. B's first and second statements are true and third statement is false. Therefore, C did not do it. A is guilty. His first statement is true; B's statements are all true; and C's first and second statements are true.

SUMMARY SOLUTION
A is guilty.

S2-19 Who Stole the Baseball Mitt?

CONSIDERATIONS
Consider that each suspect makes the same number of true and false statements.

Assume that B is the culprit. If so, B has at least two false statements, and C has at least two true statements. Therefore, B is not guilty.

Assume that C is guilty. If so, A's first and third statements are consistent with B's third and first statements. However, their second statements contradict each other; one is true and one is false. Therefore, they have different numbers of true statements. Therefore, C is not guilty.

Therefore, A did it. Each suspect has one true and two false statements.

SUMMARY SOLUTION
A did it.

S2-20 Who Stole Golf Cart No. 22?

CONSIDERATIONS
Consider that only one makes no false statements.

A's first and third statements are false, as all four were present. C's first statement agrees with A's first statement, so it too is false. D's first statement contradicts C's third statement that truthfully claims that A's third statement is false.

Therefore, the only reveler with three true statements is B. As indicated by B's second statement, C is guilty.

SUMMARY SOLUTION
C is guilty.

S2-21 Unsavory Characters

CONSIDERATIONS

Consider that the culprit makes one true and two false statements.

Assume that A is guilty. If so, all three of his statements are false. Therefore, A did not do it.

Assume that B is guilty. If so, B's first two statements are true. Therefore, B is innocent.

Assume that C is the guilty party. If so, his first and third statements are true. Therefore, C did not do it.

Therefore, D did it. His first statement is true, and second and third statements are false.

SUMMARY SOLUTION

D is guilty.

S2-22 Who Is the Shoplifter?

CONSIDERATIONS

Consider that the culprit makes three false statements; one of the other suspects makes two true and one false statement; and one makes one true and two false statements.

A's first and third statements contradict each other; one is true and one is false. Therefore, A cannot be the guilty suspect.

Assume that C is the culprit. If so, A must be the suspect with two true and one false statement, and B must be the one with one true and two false statements. However, B's third statement would be true; and B's first and second statements contradict C's first and third statements. One of B's two statements must be true and the other false. Therefore, one of C's two statements must be false and the other must be true. Therefore, C is innocent.

Therefore, B is guilty. A has made one true and two false statements; C has made two true and one false statement; and B's three statements are false.

SUMMARY SOLUTION

B is guilty.

S2-23 Who Stole the Prime Steaks?

CONSIDERATIONS

Consider that each suspect makes two true and two false statements.

Consider C's first statement. It must be false; otherwise it would be a contradiction. Consider C's third statement. Since it was a given that one of the suspects is guilty, it is false. Therefore, C's second and fourth statements are true.

Therefore, B's first statement is false, since it disagrees with C's second statement, which is true. Also, B's fourth statement is false, as A must have made two true and two false statements. Therefore, B's second and third statements are true. B is innocent.

A's second statement disagrees with C's fourth statement, which is true. Therefore, it is false. A's third statement is false, as it was a given that a truck was used in the theft. A's first and fourth statements are true. C is the thief.

SUMMARY SOLUTION

C is the thief.

S2-24 Jewelry Theft

CONSIDERATIONS

Since no two suspects make the same number of false statements, we can conclude that only one makes three true statements; one makes two true statements; one makes one true statement; and one makes no true statements.

Assume that the thief is B. If so, B's first statement is true, and second and third statements are false. However, if so, D's first and third statements are false and second statement is true. Therefore, since B and D would have the same number of true and false statements, B is not the thief.

Assume that the thief is C. If so, C's first and second statements are true and third statement is false. However, if so, D's first statement is false, and second and third statements are true. Therefore, C is innocent.

Assume D is the thief. If so, D's first statement is false, and second and third statements are true. However, if so, C's first and second statements are true and third statement is false. Therefore, D is not the thief.

Therefore, A is the thief. He makes three false statements; B makes two true and one false statement; C makes one true and two false statements; and D makes three true statements.

SUMMARY SOLUTION

A is the thief.

S2-25 Who Aced Jake the Snake?

CONSIDERATIONS

Consider that in total there are three true and three false statements.

Assume that B is guilty. If so, A makes one true statement; B makes no true statements; C makes two true statements; and D makes one true statement. Therefore, B is not guilty, as there would be four true statements.

Assume that C is guilty. If so, A makes one true statement; B makes one true statement; and D makes two true statements. Therefore, since there would be four true statements, C is innocent.

Assume that D is guilty. If so, A makes one true statement; B makes two true statements; C makes one true statement; and D makes no true statements. Therefore, D did not do it.

Therefore, A is guilty. A makes no true statements; B makes one true statement; C makes one true statement; and D makes one true statement.

SUMMARY SOLUTION
A is guilty.

S2-26 A Dead-Serious Poker Game

CONSIDERATIONS
Consider that one culprit makes two true statements and the other makes two false statements.

Assume that A is one of the two guilty players. If so, since A claims he was not involved in the game, his two statements must both be false, and D's first statement that A and C are the thieves must be true. If so, C must be the guilty player with two true statements. However, C's second statement, which claims that he wasn't in the room, is false. Therefore, A is not guilty.

Assume C is one of the two who are guilty. If so, since C's second statement is that he had stepped out of the room, he must be the guilty player with two false statements. However, we know that A is not guilty, and neither B, D, nor E makes two true statements. Therefore, C is not guilty.

Assume D is one of the two guilty players. If so, since D claims that the guilty players are A and C, D must be the thief with two false statements, and from his second statement, which must be false, E's assertion that C is not guilty must be false, and C is the second guilty player. However, since we know that C is innocent, D is not guilty.

Therefore, the two guilty players are B and E. B's statements are both false, and E's statements are both true.

SUMMARY SOLUTION

B and E are the two guilty players.

S2-27 Who Released the Desert Zoo Animals?

CONSIDERATIONS

Consider that the one who released a bobcat makes two true and one false statement; the one who released a coyote makes one true and two false statements; and the one who released a javelina and the one who released a mountain lion each make three false statements. One of the culprits also released a mountain goat and one released a gila monster.

B released the javelina and D released the mountain lion. This is apparent, as the one who released the javelina and the one who released the mountain lion make only false statements. Neither could have been the one who responded to A's first statement or C's first statement, as their answers would have been true.

From A's first statement, if true, A is the one who released the bobcat. If it is false, A is the one who released the coyote. In either case, one of A's second and third statements is true and the other is false. From A's third statement, which we know to be true, A's second statement is false. A released the mountain goat.

From B's second statement, which is false, C released the coyote and, therefore, A released the bobcat. From C's second statement, which is false, C did not release the gila monster. From B's third statement, which is false, B did not release the gila monster. From D's second statement, which is false, D did not release the gila monster. Therefore, A released the gila monster.

A   released bobcat, mountain goat, gila monster
B   released javelina
C   released coyote
D   released mountain lion

3. Fragments

S3-1a Four Vehicles

CONSIDERATIONS

From statement 1, Mr. Terrill drives a white vehicle, which is not the sedan. From statements 2 and 5, Mrs. Terrill drives the pickup truck, which is red. From statement 3, the vehicle Johnny drives to school is not the roadster, and from statement 4, since the two vehicles remaining for Johnny are the sedan and the sports utility vehicle, he drives the sports utility vehicle. (The sports utility vehicle is brand new.) It is yellow. The antique vehicle is the sedan; it is green.

Mr. Terrill	white roadster
Mrs. Terrill	red truck
Johnny	yellow sports utility vehicle
extra car	green sedan

S3-2a Halloween Costumes

CONSIDERATIONS

From statements 1 and 5, Jimmy and Molly are the Dixons. From statements 2 and 3, Billy is not Smith. Therefore, he is Finley. Therefore, Sam is Smith.

From statements 1 and 2, it was Billy Finley who wore the witch costume. Therefore, Sam wore the pirate costume. From statements 1 and 4, Jimmy wore the skeleton costume, and Molly wore the Robin Hood costume.

SUMMARY SOLUTION

Billy Finley	witch costume
Jimmy Dixon	skeleton costume
Molly Dixon	Robin Hood costume
Sam Smith	pirate costume

S3-3a Golfing Couples

CONSIDERATIONS

The average score of the four players was 93.5 strokes (187 divided by 2). Therefore, from statement 3, one of the Alberts scored 93 and the other scored 94. From statement 4, the average score of the two men was 94.5 and the average score of the two women was 92.5.

From statement 2, Kathryn's score must have been 94, and Carol's score was 91. Therefore, Kathryn's married name was Albert and, from statement 1, she was married to George, who scored 93 points. Carol Baker was married to Harry, who scored 96 points.

SUMMARY SOLUTION

Carol Baker	91 points
George Albert	93 points
Harry Baker	96 points
Kathryn Albert	94 points

S3-4a Vacation Trips

CONSIDERATIONS

From statements 1, 2, and 3, Joyce's husband is not Jack or John. Therefore, it is James. From statements

3 and 4, their surname is Adams. From statement 1, they are going to Atlanta.

From statement 5, Joan is not Abernathy. Therefore, her surname is Anderson. From statements 2 and 3, her husband is John. Their destination is Santa Barbara. Therefore, Jean and Jack Abernathy's destination is Tucson.

SUMMARY SOLUTION

Jack and Jean Abernathy	Tucson
James and Joyce Adams	Atlanta
John and Joan Anderson	Santa Barbara

S3-5a Accomplished Sisters

CONSIDERATIONS

From statements 1 and 2, the sister who plays the clarinet speaks Italian, and the one who speaks Spanish plays the piano. From statement 3, Sheri must be the sister who speaks French, and she plays either the violin or the flute. From statements 4 and 5, Ellen speaks Spanish and plays the piano, and Renee must be the sister who plays the clarinet and speaks Italian. Therefore, it is Theresa who plays the violin and speaks German, and Sheri plays the flute.

Ellen	piano	Spanish
Renee	clarinet	Italian
Sheri	flute	French
Theresa	violin	German

S3-6a Summer Fun

CONSIDERATIONS

From statements 3 and 5, Theresa and Tony were playing catch. From statement 4, Tony is not 6, and from statement 3, Tony is one of the two five-year-olds. From statements 1 and 5, Theresa is the seven-year-old. From statements 1 and 5, Ted was playing with a dog. Therefore, Timmy was flying a kite. From statement 5, Ted, who is not older than Timmy, must be the other five-year-old, and Timmy is the six-year-old.

SUMMARY SOLUTION

Ted	5 years old	playing with dog
Timmy	6 years old	kiting
Theresa	7 years old	playing catch
Tony	5 years old	playing catch

S3-7a Resort Activities

CONSIDERATIONS

From statements 2 and 4, Gene's surname is Thompson. From statement 3, Taylor, who is not Pat or Gene, is Jerry, whose activity was horseback riding. Therefore, the husband of Pat is Tyson.

From statements 1 and 5, Jerry's wife is not Pat. Therefore, his wife is Jean.

From statement 1, Gene's wife is Pat, and their activity was tennis. Therefore, Pat Tyson's wife is Geri, and their activity was golf.

SUMMARY SOLUTION

Gene and Pat Thompson	tennis
Jerry and Jean Taylor	horseback riding
Pat and Geri Tyson	golf

S3-8a Favorite Jazz Tunes

CONSIDERATIONS

From statements 1, 3, and 2, *Indiana* and *How High the Moon* are favorites of Steve and Roger, and neither *Crazy Rhythm* nor *Sunny Side of the Street* is the favorite of Ansel. Therefore, Ansel's favorite is *Lullaby of Birdland.* From statement 4, Caroline's favorite tune must be *Crazy Rhythm.*

Since Mel doesn't favor *Indiana* or *How High the Moon*, his favorite is *Sunny Side of the Street.*

From statement 5, Steve's favorite tune is *Indiana*, and Roger's favorite is *How High the Moon.*

SUMMARY SOLUTION

Ansel	*Lullaby of Birdland*
Caroline	*Crazy Rhythm*
Mel	*Sunny Side of the Street*
Roger	*How High the Moon*
Steve	*Indiana*

S3-9a Shopping at Martin's Men's Clothing

CONSIDERATIONS

From statements 1 and 5, Irwin Hill bought a dress shirt that day, and was the first of the four friends to make a purchase.

From statement 3, Harry, who bought a sport coat, was the fourth to shop. Therefore, from statements 6 and 4, Frank Goodwin was the second to shop, and from statements 6 and 2, George Matthews was the third to shop. Therefore, Harry was Thompson.

From statement 4, Frank Goodwin did not purchase socks, and we know that Irwin Hill bought a dress shirt and Harry bought a sport coat. Therefore, Frank bought a sweater and George bought socks.

SUMMARY SOLUTION

Irwin Hill	dress shirt	1st
Frank Goodwin	sweater	2nd
George Matthews	socks	3rd
Harry Thompson	sport coat	4th

S3-10a Extreme Activities

CONSIDERATIONS

From statement 4, Theresa's favorite activity is hang gliding. From statement 5, her married name is either King or Ladue. From statement 3, Mike is neither King nor Ladue. Therefore, his wife is not Theresa. From statements 3 and 5, Mike's surname is Jackson or Irvin.

From statements 1, 3, and 5, Otto is either Jackson or Irvin, and his favorite activity is not white-water rafting, hang gliding, or rock climbing. Therefore, his activity is parachute jumping. From statement 7, his wife is Vicky.

From statement 2, Nate and his wife, who are not the Kings, are the Ladues, since Mike and Otto are Irvin and Jackson, in some order. Therefore, Pete must be King. From statement 5, Nate and Pete enjoy hang gliding and white-water rafting, in some order. From statement 6, Nate Ladue and his wife, who must be Theresa, enjoy hang gliding. Therefore, Pete King and his wife favor white-water rafting. Therefore, Mike's favorite activity must be rock climbing.

From statement 4, since Ursula's surname is not Irvin or King, it must be Jackson (Theresa is Ladue), and, since Vicky's activity is parachute jumping, Ursula's must be rock climbing. Therefore, she is Mike Jackson's wife. Therefore, Vicky's husband is Otto Irvin. Therefore, Sally's surname is King and she favors white-water rafting.

SUMMARY SOLUTION

Mike and Ursula Jackson favor rock climbing.
Nate and Theresa Ladue favor hang gliding.
Otto and Vicky Irvin favor parachute jumping.
Pete and Sally King favor white-water rafting.

S3-11a College Reunion

CONSIDERATIONS

From statements 2 and 5, Jim is Morrison and Jerry is Mahoney. From statement 3, Joe, who isn't Mayer, is Mason. Therefore, Jamie is Mayer, the computer programmer.

From statement 6, Jerry, who isn't the lawyer, the financial consultant, or the computer programmer, is the dentist, and, from statement 4, he was a quarterback.

From statement 1, Joe Mason was not a defensive end or a center, and since he wasn't a quarterback, he was a linebacker. From statement 4, Joe is the financial consultant. Therefore, Jim Morrison is the lawyer. Therefore, he was a defensive end, and Jamie Mayer was a center.

SUMMARY SOLUTION

Jamie Mayer	center	computer programmer
Jerry Mahoney	quarterback	dentist
Jim Morrison	defensive end	lawyer
Joe Mason	linebacker	financial consultant

S3-12a Dancing Couples

CONSIDERATIONS

From statements 1, 4, and 5, Walt's surname is not Campbell, Conway, or Cole. Therefore, his surname is Carlson. From statement 2, Walt's preferred dance is either the rumba or cha-cha. From statements 3, 4, 6, and 8, Walt's wife is not Anne, Betty, or Shirley. Therefore, his wife is Gloria.

From statement 3, Anne prefers the waltz. Therefore, from statement 2, Anne's surname is either Cole or Conway, and from statement 7, Anne's surname is Conway.

From statements 5 and 6, Betty's surname is Cole, and from statement 2, her preferred dance is swing.

Shirley's surname must be either Carlson or Campbell. From statement 8, Shirley is Campbell, and the cha-cha is her preferred dance. Therefore, Walt and Gloria's preferred dance is the rumba.

From statements 4 and 5, Tom is not Conway or Cole, and since Walt is Carson, Tom is Campbell, his wife is Shirley, and his preferred dance is the cha-cha.

From statement 1, Stan does not prefer swing, so his preferred dance is the waltz, his wife is Anne, and his surname is Conway. Therefore, Sam's wife is Betty Cole, whose preferred dance is swing.

SUMMARY SOLUTION

Sam and Betty Cole	swing
Stan and Anne Conway	waltz
Sam and Shirley Campbell	cha-cha
Walt and Gloria Carlson	rumba

S3-13a Favorite Outdoor Recreation

CONSIDERATIONS

From statements 1, 3, and 4, Ginger and her husband's preferred recreation is not golf, hiking, sailing, or fly-fishing. Therefore, their recreation is tennis. From statement 5, Ginger's married name is Lane. From statement 2, Ginger's husband is Bob.

From statements 6, 1, and 4, Joyce's husband is not Conrad, Doug, or Al. Also, we know her husband is not Bob. Therefore, her husband is Ed, and their recreational interest is golf. From statement 2, Ed and Joyce are not the Nadlers, Owens, or Kelsos. Also, we know they are not the Lanes. Therefore, Ed and Joyce are the Markhams.

From statement 4, Al and his wife, who is not Irma or Ginger, enjoy fly-fishing. From statement 3, Al's wife is not Fran. Also, from statement 6, Al's wife is not Joyce. Therefore, Al's wife is Harriet. From state-ments 2 and 7, Al and Harriet are the Nadlers.

From statements 2 and 8, Conrad and his wife are the Kelsos. Their recreational interest is hiking. From statement 3, Conrad's wife is not Fran. Therefore, she is Irma. Therefore, Doug and Fran Owens enjoy sailing.

SUMMARY SOLUTION

Al and Harriet Nadler	fly-fishing
Bob and Ginger Lane	tennis
Conrad and Irma Kelso	hiking
Doug and Fran Owens	sailing
Ed and Joyce Markham	golf

S3-14a Neighbors' Houses

CONSIDERATIONS

From statements 1 and 2, we can conclude that the Quigley house is one of at least three houses on its side of the street.

From statement 5, the Unger and the Smith houses are the two on the south side of the street. The Unger house is at the west end of the street, and is white. The Smith house is either green or blue.

From statement 3, the Rodneys and the Quigleys are two of the three neighbors that live on the north side of the street. From statements 4 and 6, the Taylor house is between the Rodney and the Quigley house and is blue. The Rodneys live in the second white house. The Smith house is green and the Quigley house is gray.

SUMMARY SOLUTION

Quigley	north side	gray
Rodney	north side	white
Smith	south side	green
Taylor	north side	blue
Unger	south side	white

S3-15a Tennis Tournament

CONSIDERATIONS

From statements 1 and 4, Jack Ernst and Phil play for Skyview Country Club. From statements 4 and 6, Donald Farrell is playing in the men's singles for Mountainside Country Club. From statements 4 and 6, Phil Hartland is in the mixed doubles for Skyline Country Club. Therefore, Jack Ernst is in the men's doubles.

From statements 1, 2, and 5, Anne Irwin is playing in the women's singles for Mountainside Country Club. From statements 2 and 6, Claire Gardner is playing in the mixed-doubles event for Skyline Country Club. Therefore, Ruth Dixon is playing in the women's doubles for Mountainside Country Club.

SUMMARY SOLUTION

Anne Irwin	women's singles	Mountainside
Claire Gardner	mixed doubles	Skyline
Donald Farrell	men's singles	Mountainside
Jack Ernst	men's doubles	Skyline
Phil Hartland	mixed doubles	Skyline
Ruth Dixon	women's doubles	Mountainside

S3-16a Bridge Players

CONSIDERATIONS

From statement 5, Mrs. Smith's partner was her daughter, either Mrs. Johnson, Mrs. Jones, or Mrs. Williams. From statement 1, Mrs. Johnson's partner was her son-in-law, and from statement 6, Mrs. Williams's partner was her grandfather. Therefore, Mrs. Smith's partner was Mrs. Jones.

From statement 6, Mrs. Williams's partner was her

grandfather, who was Mr. Jones, Mr. Smith, or Mr. Johnson. From statement 2, Mr. Jones's partner was his brother-in-law, and from statement 7, Mr. Johnson's partner was a man. Therefore, Mrs. Williams's partner was Mr. Smith.

From statement 1, Mrs. Johnson's partner was her son-in-law, who was Mr. Jones, Mr. Smith, or Mr. Williams. We know that Mr. Jones's partner was his wife's brother-in-law, and Mr. Smith's partner was Mrs. Williams. Therefore, Mrs. Johnson's partner was Mr. Williams. Therefore, Mr. Jones and Mr. Johnson were partners.

From statement 4, Mr. Johnson and his partner, Mr. Jones, played against his father-in-law, who is Mr. Smith (Mrs. Smith's daughter is Mrs. Jones), and Mrs. Williams at the first table. From statement 3, Mrs. Jones, who partnered with Mrs. Smith, played against her sister, Mrs. Johnson, and Mr. Williams at the other table.

SUMMARY SOLUTION

Table 1: Mr. Smith and Mrs. Williams played against Mr. Johnson and Mr. Jones.

Table 2: Mrs. Smith and Mrs. Jones played against Mr. Williams and Mrs. Johnson.

S3-17a African Safari

CONSIDERATIONS

From statements 1 and 9, Vern's surname is Dewitt and Dan's surname is Duffy. From statement 6, Dan sighted a leopard.

From statement 7, the Lundstroms and the Duffys were the two couples who traveled together often. From statement 2, Margo and Eve, Lois, or Tina are Mrs. Lundstrom and Mrs. Duffy, in some order.

From statement 10, Margo and Mark are the Lundstroms and he sighted a zebra. From statement 5, Margo sighted a giraffe. From statements 3 and 6, Eve is not Mrs. Duffy.

From statements 4 and 11, Lois is not Mrs. Duffy. Therefore, Tina is Mrs. Duffy. From statement 6, Tina's animal was a wildebeest. From statements 1, 4, and 8, Vern Dewitt's animal was a hyena.

Tom's surname must be Mueller. From statement 12, his wife is Lois. Eve is Mrs. Dewitt, who was first to sight a lion.

From statement 9, Tom wasn't the first to spot a cheetah, so Lois was. Tom was first to spot an elephant.

SUMMARY SOLUTION

Dan Duffy	leopard
Tina Duffy	wildebeest
Mark Lundstrom	zebra
Margo Lundstrom	giraffe
Tom Mueller	elephant
Lois Mueller	cheetah
Vern Dewitt	hyena
Eve Dewitt	lion

S3-18a The Father-and-Son Campout

CONSIDERATIONS

From statement 5, Chuck and Eddie are the two oldest boys. Therefore, one of them is 11 and the other is one of the ten-year-olds.

From statement 4, Jeff's son is 11, 10, or 9. From statements 1 and 2, Jeff's son is not 11 or 10. Therefore, he is 9 years old.

From statement 2, Mr. Grayson's son is one of the ten-year-olds, and from statement 3, Mr. Dudley's son is the other ten-year-old. Therefore, from statements 3 and 4, Mr. Jackson's son must be Eddie, who is 11 years old. Therefore, Chuck is one of the two ten-year-olds. Mr. Jackson is not Bill, George, Jeff, or James; he must be David.

From statement 7, since Chuck is not Mr. Grayson's son, he must be Mr. Dudley's son, and from statement 3, Mr. Dudley is James.

From statement 5, Ned and Gary are the two youngest boys. Therefore, one of them is 9 years old and the other is 9½. Therefore, Rickie must be the other ten-year-old and the son of Mr. Grayson. From statement 6, since Gary's father is not Mr. Bradley, he must be Mr. Albertson. Therefore, Ned's surname is Bradley.

From statement 7, since George is not Mr. Grayson or Mr. Bradley, he must be Mr. Albertson, Gary's father, and Jeff Bradley is Ned's father. Ned is 9 years old, and Gary is 9½.

Bill is Rickie's father.

SUMMARY SOLUTION

Chuck Dudley	10	son of James
Eddie Jackson	11	son of David
Gary Albertson	9½	son of George
Ned Bradley	9	son of Jeff
Rickie Grayson	10	son of Bill

S3-19a Knowheyan Physical Characteristics

CONSIDERATIONS

From statements 2, 3, and 6, C is younger than A, D, and E. Therefore, since none of the three is 280 Knowheyan years old, C is 200 years old. Therefore, B is 280 years old.

From statement 3, A, D, or C does not have black hair. Therefore, either B or E has black hair. From statements 8 and 7, since E is taller than the one with golden hair, who is taller than the one with black hair, B is the one with black hair and must be 3 meters or 3.25 meters tall. From statement 1, he's 3 meters tall.

From statements 8 and 7, the one with orange hair must be 3.75 meters or 4 meters tall and the one with golden hair must be 3.25 or 3.5 meters tall. From statements 4 and 5, the one with silver hair is not 3.5 meters, 3.75 meters, or 4 meters tall. Since B, who has black hair, is 3 meters tall, the one with silver hair is 3.25 meters tall. From statement 8, E is taller than the one with golden hair and shorter than the one with orange hair. Therefore, E is 3.75 meters tall and the one with orange hair is 4 meters tall. Therefore, E has red hair, since 3.75 meters is the remaining height for the one with red hair.

From statement 6, C is not the one who is 3.5 meters tall. Therefore, since B is 3 meters tall and E is 3.75 meters tall, C must be either 3.25 meters tall or 4 meters tall. However, from statement 5, the one who has silver hair, who is 3.25 meters tall, is older than C, who is the youngest of the five inhabitants. Therefore, C is 4 meters tall and has orange hair.

From statement 8, the one who has golden hair, who is 3.5 meters tall, is not 240 years old. The one who is 240 years old must be 3.25 meters tall or 3.75 meters tall. Also, from statement 8, E, who is 3.75 meters tall, is taller than the one who is 240 years old. Therefore, the one who is 240 years old is 3.25 meters tall and has silver hair. Therefore, E, who is 3.75 meters tall and has red hair, is 220 years old.

Therefore, A is 240 years old, has silver hair, and is 3.25 meters tall. D is 260 years old, is 3.5 meters tall, and has golden hair.

SUMMARY SOLUTION

A	3.25 m.	240 years	silver hair
B	3 m.	280 years	black hair
C	4 m.	200 years	orange hair
D	3.5 m.	260 years	golden hair
E	3.75 m.	220 years	red hair

S3-20a Fishing Tournament

CONSIDERATIONS

Since three anglers won the four categories, one of them won two categories and earned a bonus point. Since there were two winners, the only possibility is that they each received four points. One won the total-weight category (4 points); the other won the largest-fish category (2 points) and the second-largest-fish category (1 point) and, in addition, received the bonus point for winning two categories.

From statements 2, 4, and 5, neither McNess, Larson, nor Smith used a spinner bait. From statement 6, Jones could not have won both the most-fish category and, from statement 5, the largest-fish category (his total points would have exceeded 4). Therefore, Jones did not use a spinner bait. Therefore, Black used a spinner bait and, from statement 5, won the largest-fish category and the second-largest-fish category, as well as the bonus point, for a total of 4 points. From statements 1, 2, and 4, Black's first name is not Mike, Terry, Vick, or Sam. Therefore, Black's first name is Kevin.

From statements 4, 6, and 7, neither Larson, Jones, nor McNess used a deep-running crank bait. Therefore, since we know that Black used a spinner bait, Smith must have used a deep-running crank bait.

From statements 1 and 4, neither Sam nor Larson used a plastic worm or a spinner bait. Therefore, one used a weighted jig and one used a wounded-minnow bait. From statement 1, Mike did not use a plastic worm; and, since Sam and Larson used a weighted jig and a wounded-minnow bait, and Kevin used a spinner bait, Mike used a deep-running crank bait. Therefore, Mike is Smith. From statement 6, Mike did not catch the most fish. Therefore, from statement 1, Mike won the total-weight category and received four points.

From statements 3 and 7, Terry did not use a weighted jig or a plastic worm. Therefore, Terry used a wounded-minnow bait. Therefore, Terry is Larson. Sam used a weighted jig and, from statement 3, did not win a category, so received no points. Since, from statement 6, Jones caught the most fish, Sam is McNess. Therefore, Vick is Jones, used a plastic worm, caught the most fish, and received three points. Terry Larson did not win a category, so received no points.

SUMMARY SOLUTION

Kevin Black: spinner bait, largest fish and second-largest fish, 4 points

Mike Smith: crank bait, total weight, 4 points
Sam McNess: weighted jig, no category, 0 points
Terry Larson; wounded-minnow bait, no category, 0
   points
Vick Jones: plastic worm, most fish, 3 points

Kevin and Mike tied for first place.

S3-21b Lost in Rome and Paris

CONSIDERATIONS

Consider that one of the statements is false.

From statement 1, Eleanor did not come upon the Sistine Chapel, the Trevi Fountain, or St. Peter's Basilica. From statement 6, either Betty or Frances came upon the Colosseum. From these two statements, Eleanor did not come upon any of the four sights in Rome. Therefore, one of these statements is false.

Assume that statement 6 is the false statement. If so, Eleanor must have come upon the Colosseum. If so, from statement 3, Eleanor must have come upon the Eiffel Tower, and from statement 4, Frances must have come upon the Notre Dame Cathedral. However, from statement 2, Frances came upon either the

Eiffel Tower or the Moulin Rouge Cabaret. Therefore, statement 1 is the false statement.

From statement 5, Betty came upon either the Sistine Chapel or the Colosseum; and from statement 9, Betty or Helena came upon St. Peter's Basilica. Therefore, Helena came upon St. Peter's Basilica. From statements 3 and 8, Helena came upon the Louvre Museum. From statements 2, 3, 5, and 7, Frances came upon the Colosseum and Betty came upon the Sistine Chapel.

Eleanor came upon the Trevi Fountain and, from statement 4, the Notre Dame Cathedral. From statement 8, Helena came upon the Louvre Museum. From statement 7, Betty came upon the Moulin Rouge Cabaret.

SUMMARY SOLUTION

Eleanor	Trevi Fountain	Notre Dame Cathedral
Frances	Colosseum	Eiffel Tower
Betty	Sistine Chapel	Moulin Rouge Cabaret
Helena	St Peter's Basilica	Louvre Museum

S3-22b Orange Pickers

CONSIDERATIONS

Consider that one statement is false.

From statements 2, 4, and 5, it appears that no one received the first-place bonus as having picked the most fruit. Therefore, one of these three statements must be false. From statement 1, neither Bob nor Chad picked the most. Therefore, either Deek or Evan did. From statement 1, Deek picked more than Bob, and from statement 6, Bob's and Evan's amounts were so close their positions had to be settled by a coin toss. Therefore, Deek picked the most, and statement 4 is the false statement.

From statements 6 and 7, Bob won the third-place bonus and Chad is Taylor. Also, Evan is Wagner, who earned the second-place bonus. From statement 6, Bob, who is not Unger, is Smith. Therefore, Deek is Unger.

SUMMARY SOLUTION

Deek Unger	1st
Evan Wagner	2nd
Bob Smith	3rd
Chad Taylor	4th

S-3-23b Apartment Dwellers

CONSIDERATIONS

One statement is false.

From statement 2, Keith lives below Kathleen and Kevin. From statement 5, Keith lives on the 17th floor. These two statements are inconsistent. One of statements 2 and 5 is false. From statement 1, Carl lives three floors above Keith. However, from statement 6, Carl does not live on the 20th floor. Therefore, Carl must live on the 15th floor and Keith lives on the 12th floor. Therefore, statement 5 is false.

From statement 7, Cathy and Kathy live on the 5th and 10th floors, in some order. From statement 4, Kathy lives on the 10th floor and Cathy lives on the 5th floor. From statement 3, Kathleen lives on the 20th floor and Kevin lives on the 17th floor.

SUMMARY SOLUTION

Carl	15th floor
Cathy	5th floor
Kathy	10th floor
Keith	12th floor
Kevin	17th floor
Kathleen	20th floor

S3-24b Goldie Locks and the Three Bears

CONSIDERATIONS

Again, one statement is false.

From statements 2, 5, and 7, it appears that none of the four children selected for the play was cast to play the Goldie Locks character. Therefore, one of these three statements is false. From statement 1, Mike, Pat, and Del are not related. Therefore, Dale must be related to one of the three. From statement 6, Dale, who is not Farrell or Ford, is Foster. From statement 4, neither Mike nor Pat is Foster. Therefore, Del is Foster, and Dale's sibling. Therefore, statement 2, which indicates that Dale and Del met for the first time in school, is the false statement.

From statements 3, 1, and 7, Del Foster was cast as Mama Bear, Mike Farrell was cast as Baby Bear, and Pat Ford was cast as Papa Bear. Therefore, Dale Foster was cast as Goldie Locks.

SUMMARY SOLUTION

Dale Foster	Goldie Locks
Del Foster	Mama Bear
Mike Farrell	Baby Bear
Pat Ford	Papa Bear

S3-25b High-School Basketball Team

CONSIDERATIONS

One statement is false.

From statements 2 and 4, the center must be Joe. However, from statement 7, Joe is not the center. One of statements 2, 4, and 7 is false. Statement 5 indicates that Joe is neither one of the forwards nor one of the guards. Considered along with statement 7, there is no position left for Joe. Therefore, statement 7 is false; Joe must be the center.

From statements 3 and 6, the sixth man is James. From statements 1 and 3, Jake, who is a sophomore, is one of the guards. From statement 6, Johnny is the other guard. Therefore, the two forwards are Jerome and Jim.

SUMMARY SOLUTION

Jake	guard
James	sixth man
Jerome	forward
Jim	forward
Joe	center
Johnny	guard

S3-26b State High-School Baseball Championship

CONSIDERATIONS

One statement is false.

From statement 1, since the Bears did not meet the Wildcats in one semifinal game, they must have met either the Lions or the Cardinals. From statement 2, they did not meet the Cardinals. Therefore, they must have met the Lions. However, from statement 3, they did not meet the Lions. One of statements 1, 2, and 3 is false.

From statements 4 and 6, the Bears did not meet the Lions. This is consistent with statement 3. From statements 4 and 5, since neither the Bears nor the Lions were in the championship game, and the team that the Wildcats beat was not the Lions, then it was the Bears. Therefore, statement 1 is the false statement.

From statement 6, the Cardinals must have been the team that beat the Lions and won the State championship.

SUMMARY SOLUTION

The Lions met the Cardinals in one semifinal game. The Bears met the Wildcats in the other semifinal game. The Cardinals and the Wildcats met in the final game. The Wildcats won the championship.

S3-27b Couples' Dinners

CONSIDERATIONS

Consider that one statement is false.

Statement 3 indicates that Harriet's spouse is either Carl or Al. Statements 1 and 2 indicate other wives for Al and Carl. One of statements 1, 2, and 3 is false. From statement 3, Harriet is a newlywed. From statement 5, the Thomases have been married the shortest time. Assume that statement 2 is the false statement. From statements 3 and 5, Carl is not Thomas, who has been married the shortest length of time. This is inconsistent with statement 3. Assume that statement 1 is the false statement. From statement 6, Al and his wife have been married longer than the Tuckers, which is also inconsistent with statement 3. Therefore, statement 3 is the false statement. Harriet is married to Bart.

From statements 1, 5, and 6, Al and Fran are not the Thomases or the Tuckers. Therefore, they are the Taylors. From statement 4, Carl is not Thomas. Therefore, from statement 2, Eileen and Carl are the Tuckers. Therefore, Bert and Harriet are the Thomases.

SUMMARY SOLUTION

Al and Fran Taylor
Bert and Harriet Thomas
Carl and Eileen Tucker

S3-28b Active New Zealand Vacations

CONSIDERATIONS

One statement is false.

From statement 1, June and Sam are married. From statement 4, June and Jenny are neighbors. From statement 7, Sam doesn't live near the others. Therefore, one of statements 1, 4, and 7 must be false. Statement 4 is also contradictory with statement 6. Therefore, statement 4 is false.

From statements 1, 7, and 3, June and Sam Holt are the couple who enjoy trekking. From statements 5, 8, and 2, Terry Hart's primary New Zealand interest is fly-fishing. Therefore, Patrick Hunt's interest is the exciting activities. From statement 1, Jenny's interest is the exciting activities. Therefore, she is Hunt; and Kathy Hart's interest is fly-fishing.

Patrick and Jenny Hunt	exciting activities
Sam and June Holt	trekking
Terry and Kathy Hart	fly-fishing

S3-29b The Forest People

CONSIDERATIONS

One statement is false.

From statement 1, Har was not the oldest or tallest. From statement 5, Har was taller than Winn and Tolo. From statement 2, Winn was taller than Edvo and Frer, which would make Har the tallest of the forest people. Therefore, one of statements 1, 2, and 5 is false. From statement 3, Tolo was older than Har, which contradicts statement 5. Therefore, statement 5 is false.

From statements 1, 2, and 3, Har was not the shortest or the tallest, and Winn was taller than Edvo, Frer, and Tolo. Therefore, Winn was the tallest: sixteen hands. Since Tolo was shorter than Frer or Edvo, Tolo was the shortest: twelve hands. Since Har was not the oldest, from statement 4, he was not thirteen hands tall. Therefore, Frer, who was shorter than Edvo (statement 2), was thirteen hands tall and he was the oldest.

From statements 3 and 6, Tolo was not the second oldest, the fourth oldest, or the youngest. Therefore, Tolo was the third oldest: 120 years. Also, from statement 6, Edvo was not the fourth oldest or the youngest. Therefore, Edvo was the second oldest: 130 years. Since the fourth oldest was shorter than Edvo, Har must have been the fourth oldest: 110 years; and Winn was the youngest: 100 years. Since the fourth oldest was shorter than Edvo, Har was fourteen hands and Edvo was fifteen hands.

SUMMARY SOLUTION

Edvo	fifteen hands	130 years
Frer	thirteen hands	140 years
Har	fourteen hands	110 years
Tolo	twelve hands	120 years
Winn	sixteen hands	100 years

S3-30b Tree Plantings

CONSIDERATIONS

One statement is false.

From statements 1, 2, 3, and 4, Ken, Doug, Ted,

Art, and Gene are not Jacobs. Therefore, since one of the five neighbors is Jacobs, we can conclude that one of these four statements is false.

From statements 8 and 10, Art is not Waldron. From statements 3 and 8, both Art and Waldron planted white oaks. Therefore, since each neighbor planted a different variety of tree, statement 3 is the false one.

Therefore, Art is Jacobs. From statements 2 and 8, Ted is not Waldron; from statement 7, Ted is not Bagnall; and from statement 9, since Art Jacob's immediate neighbors are Ken and Doug (statement 1), Ted is not Egan. Therefore, Ted's surname is West. Since Ken lives to the left of Art Jacobs (statement 1), from statement 8, Ken is not Waldron. If Doug were Waldron, Gene would live next to Ted West. From statement 4, this is not the case. Therefore, Doug is not Waldron. Therefore, Gene's surname is Waldron. From statement 9, Egan lives between Art Jacobs and Gene Waldron. Therefore, Doug, who lives on Art's right, is Egan. Therefore, Ken's surname is Bagnall. The relative positions of the five neighbors on the block are, as follows: Ted West, Ken Bagnall, Art Jacobs, Doug Egan, and Gene Waldron.

From statement 2, quaking aspens were planted by

Ted's neighbor, Ken Bagnall. From statement 6, Art planted water birches. From statement 9, Ted planted bigleaf maples. Therefore, Doug planted blue spruces.

SUMMARY SOLUTION

Art Jacobs	water birches
Doug Egan	blue spruces
Gene Waldron	white oaks
Ken Bagnall	quaking aspens
Ted West	bigleaf maples

S3-31c Golfers' Handicaps

CONSIDERATIONS

Only one statement is true.

Assume that statement 1 is the true statement. If so, Alice's handicap is 14 or 18. If so, statement 2 is false and Carol's handicap is 14 (lower then Alice's), but it cannot be both 14 and higher than Diane's. Therefore, statement 1 is false; Alice's handicap must be 26 or 22 (the highest or next to the highest).

Assume that statement 2 is the true statement. If so, Carol's handicap is 18 or 22 (higher than Alice's and lower than Diane's). However, since we know that Alice's handicap is 22 or 26, it is not possible for Carol's handicap to be both higher than Alice's and lower than Diane's. Therefore, statement 2 is false.

Assume that statement 4 is true. If so, Diane's handicap is 26 (higher than Alice's). However, from statement 2, which is false, Carol's handicap is higher than Diane's, which is impossible. Therefore, statement 4 is false.

Therefore, statement 3 is the true statement. Beth's handicap is 26; Alice's handicap is 22; Carol's handicap is 18; and Diane's handicap is 14.

SUMMARY SOLUTION

Alice 22
Beth   26
Carol 18
Diane 14

S3-32 Football Players

CONSIDERATIONS

Only one statement is true.

Assume statement 1 is true. If so, if Charley is not a running back then Mike is the quarterback; or else, if Charley is a running back Mike is not the quarterback. If true, from statement 2, Buddy is not the quarterback. From statement 3, either Mike or Jamey, or both, are running backs. From statement 4, neither Charley nor Buddy is the wide receiver.

From the first part of statement 1, if true, Mike is the quarterback, and the wide receiver is Charley. However, then statement 4 would also be true.

From the second part of statement 1, if Charley is a running back either Mike or Jamey is a running back. Buddy is neither the quarterback nor the wide receiver (from statements 2 and 4). In which case, there is no position for Buddy. Therefore, statement 1 must be false.

Assume that statement 2 is true. If so, Buddy is the quarterback. Again, from statement 3, either or both Mike and Jamey are running backs. From statement 4, the wide receiver is not Charley. Therefore, if statement 2 is the true statement, Mike or Jamey must be one of the running backs, and the other is Charley. However, that makes statement 1 true. Therefore, statement 2 is false.

Assume that statement 4 is true. If so, either Charley or Buddy is the wide receiver. Assume Charley is the wide receiver. If so, since statement 1 is false, the quarterback is not Mike. However, from statement 3, which is false, Mike is one of the two running backs.

Therefore, if statement 4 is true, Buddy is the wide receiver. If so, from statement 3, Mike and Jamey are the two running backs. Charlie must be the quarterback. But that makes statement 1 true. Therefore, statement 4 is false.

Therefore, statement 3 is true. Mike is the quarterback, Jamey is the wide receiver, and Charley and Buddy are the two running backs.

SUMMARY SOLUTION

Buddy	running back
Charley	running back
Jamey	wide receiver
Mike	quarterback

S3-33c Cloud Formations

CONSIDERATIONS

Only one statement is true.

Assume that statement 1 is the true statement. If so, since Charlie did not see an alligator or a rabbit, those two animals must have been seen by two of Andy, Becky, and Diane. If so, from statement 3, which would be false, Becky saw a flock of sheep.

From statement 4, which would be false, neither Andy nor Diane spotted an alligator. Therefore, statement 1 is not the true statement.

Assume statement 3 is true. If so, Becky did not spot the flock of sheep. If not, the flock of sheep was spotted by Charley, Diane, or Andy. From statement 1, which we know to be false, Charlie spotted an alligator or a rabbit; and from statement 4, which would be false, neither Andy nor Diane spotted a flock of sheep. Therefore, statement 3 is false.

Assume statement 4 is the true one. If so, Andy's and Diane's cloud formations were an alligator and a flock of sheep, in some order. If so, the lion and the rabbit must have been seen by Becky and Charlie. However, from statement 2, which would be false, Charlie did not spot the lion, and from statement 3, Becky saw the flock of sheep. Therefore, statement 4 is false.

Therefore, statement 2 is the true statement. Either Diane or Charlie saw a lion. From statement 1, Charlie saw either an alligator or a rabbit. Therefore, Diane saw the lion. From statement 3, Becky spotted the flock of sheep. From statement 4, Andy did not spot the alligator. Therefore, he spotted the rabbit, and Charlie spotted the alligator.

SUMMARY SOLUTION

Andy   rabbit
Becky   flock of sheep
Charlie   alligator
Diane   lion

S3-34c Puzzle Challenges

CONSIDERATIONS

Only one statement is true.

Assume that statement 1 is the true statement. If so, mathematical puzzles or crossword puzzles are preferred by Bill, and jigsaw puzzles are preferred by Bea. If so, logic puzzles must be favored by either Betty or Barney. However, statement 2 would have to be false. Therefore, statement 1 is false.

Assume that statement 2 is true. If so, either Barney or Betty favor logic puzzles. If so, from statement 4, which would be false, neither Betty nor Bill prefer logic puzzles, and from statement 3, which would be false, jigsaw puzzles are not preferred by either Betty, Bea, or Bill; Barney must be the one who favors jigsaw puzzles. Therefore, statement 2 is false.

Assume that statement 3 is true. If so, jigsaw puzzles are preferred by Betty, Bea, or Bill. If so, Barney does not prefer jigsaw puzzles and must prefer crossword, mathematical, or logic puzzles. From statement 2, which is false, Barney does not prefer logic puzzles. From statement 5, which would be false, Barney prefers logic puzzles or jigsaw puzzles. Therefore, statement 3 is false.

Assume that statement 5 is true. If so, Barney prefers either crossword puzzles or mathematical puzzles. If so, from statement 3, which is false, Betty, Bea, and Bill do not prefer jigsaw puzzles. Therefore, statement 5 is false.

Therefore, statement 4 is the true statement. Logic puzzles are favored by either Betty or Bill. From statement 2, which is false, Betty does not prefer logic puzzles; she prefers mathematical puzzles. Bill prefers logic puzzles. From statement 5, Barney prefers jigsaw puzzles. Therefore, Bea prefers crossword puzzles.

SUMMARY SOLUTION

Barney   jigsaw puzzles
Bea   crossword puzzles
Betty   mathematical puzzles
Bill   logic puzzles

CONSIDERATIONS

Only one statement is true.

Assume that statement 1 is the true statement. If so, Bill won the A flight; Dan won the B flight; and Charlie must have won the C flight. However, from statement 2, which would be false, Charlie did not win the C flight. Therefore, statement 1 is false. Bill did not win the A flight and/or Dan did not win the B flight.

Assume statement 2 is the true statement. If so, Charlie won the C flight. However, from statement 3, which would be false, Bill must have won the C flight. Therefore, statement 2 is false. Charlie did not win the C flight; he won either the A or the B flight.

Assume statement 4 is the true statement. If so, neither Charlie nor Dan won the A flight. However, this would mean that Bill won the A flight. From statement 3, which would be false, Bill won the C flight. Therefore, statement 4 is false.

Therefore, statement 3 is the true statement. Bill did not win the C flight. From statement 2, since we know that Charlie did not win the C flight, Dan won the C flight. From statement 4, which is false, Charlie won the A flight, and Bill won the B flight.

Bill   B flight
Charlie   A flight
Dan   C flight

S3-26c Four Vocations

CONSIDERATIONS

Only one statement is true.

Assume that statement 1 is the one true clue. If so, Mr. Carpenter is the baker. If so, from statement 4, Mr. Cook is not the carpenter. Therefore, he must be the butcher. However, from statement 3, the butcher must be Mr. Baker. Therefore, statement 1 is false.

Assume that statement 3 is true. If so, since the butcher is neither Mr. Baker nor Mr. Carpenter, Mr. Cook must be the butcher. If so, from statement 1, Mr. Carpenter is not the baker, and from statement 2, the cook must be either Mr. Butcher or Mr. Baker. Therefore, that leaves Mr. Carpenter with the vocation of carpenter—not possible. Therefore, statement 3 is false.

Assume statement 4 is true. If so, Mr. Cook is the carpenter. If so, from statement 1, Mr. Carpenter is not the baker, and from statement 2, the cook must be either Mr. Butcher or Mr. Baker. Therefore, Mr. Carpenter must be the butcher. From statement 5, Mr. Butcher is not the baker, and therefore must be the cook, which leaves Mr. Baker as the baker—not possible. Therefore, statement 4 is false.

Assume statement 5 is true. If so, Mr. Butcher is the baker. If so, from statement 2, Mr. Carpenter is not the cook. Therefore, he must be the butcher. From statement 4, Mr. Cook is not the carpenter, which leaves him the remaining vocation, cook—not possible. Therefore, statement 5 is false.

Therefore, statement 2 is the true one. Mr. Carpenter is the cook. From statement 3, Mr. Baker is the butcher. From statement 5, Mr. Butcher, who is not the baker, is the carpenter, and Mr. Cook is the baker.

SUMMARY SOLUTION

Mr. Baker	butcher
Mr. Butcher	carpenter
Mr. Cook	baker
Mr. Carpenter	cook

S3-37c Friends and Cats

CONSIDERATIONS

Only one statement is true.

Assume that statement 2 is true. If so, Betsy's cat is named Alice. If so, Dody's cat must be named Betsy or Candy. However, from statement 3, which would be false, Dody does not own either Candy or Betsy. Therefore, statement 2 is false; Betsy's cat is named either Dody or Candy.

Assume statement 3 is the true statement. If so, Dody's cat is named Candy or Betsy. From statement 1, which is false, Candy's cat must be Betsy, so Dody's is Candy. If so, Alice's cat must be named Dody. However, from statement 4, which would be false, Alice's cat is named Betsy or Candy. Therefore, statement 3 is false; Dody's cat is not named Candy or Betsy. Her cat must be named Alice.

Assume that statement 4 is the true statement. If so, Alice's cat is not named Betsy or Candy. If not, Alice's cat must be named Dody. However, from statement 5, which would be false, the cat named Dody belongs to either Candy or Betsy. Therefore, statement 4 is false; Alice's cat is named Betsy or Candy.

Assume that statement 5 is the true statement. If so, the cat named Dody does not belong to Candy or Betsy. If not, the cat named Dody must belong to Alice. However, from statement 4, which is false, Alice's cat is either Betsy or Candy.

Therefore, statement 1 is the true statement. Candy owns Dody or Alice. We know from statement 3, which is false, that Dody's cat is named Alice. Therefore, Candy's cat is Dody. From statement 2, which is false, we know that Betsy's cat is named Dody or Candy. Therefore, Betsy's cat is named Candy. Therefore, Alice's cat is named Betsy.

SUMMARY SOLUTION

Alice's cat is Betsy.
Betsy's cat is Candy.
Candy's cat is Dody.
Dody's cat is Alice.

S3-38c The Mountaintop Hermits

CONSIDERATIONS

Only one statement is true.

Assume that statement 2 is the true statement. If so, the brothers' summer meetings must have been either at the shelter that faced east or the shelter that faced west. If so, from statement 4, which would be false, their summer meetings must have been at either Homer's or Billy's shelter. However, from statement 3, which would be false, neither Homer's nor Billy's shelters faced east or west. Therefore, statement 2 is false.

Assume that statement 3 is true. If so, the shelters of Billy and Homer faced east and west, in some order. However, from statement 1, which would be false, Billy's shelter faced south. Therefore, statement 3 is false.

Assume that statement 4 is the true one. If so, their summer meetings were either at Jacob's or Willy's shelter. However, from statement 2, which is false, their summer meetings were at either the shelter that faced north or the one that faced east. From statement 3, which is false, neither Billy nor Homer lived in a shelter facing north or south. Therefore, Jacob and Willy lived in shelters that faced north and south, in some order. Therefore, statement 4 is false.

Assume that statement 5 is the true one. If so, Jacob's shelter faced south. However, from statement 3, which we know to be false, Jacob lived in a shelter facing east or west. Therefore, statement 5 is false.

Therefore, statement 1 is the true statement. From statement 1 (true) and statement 3 (false), Billy's shelter faced north, and Homer's shelter faced south. Homer hosted the spring meeting. From statement 4 (false), Billy hosted the summer meeting.

From statement 5 (false), Jacob hosted the winter meeting. Therefore, Willy hosted the fall meeting. From statement 4 (false), Willy's shelter faced east. Therefore, Jacob faced west.

SUMMARY SOLUTION

Billy	north	summer
Homer	south	spring
Jacob	west	winter
Willy	east	fall

S3-39c Sailboat Race

CONSIDERATIONS

Only one statement is true.

Assume that statement 1 is the true statement. If so, the Steinbergs must have finished in fourth or fifth place. From statement 6, which would be false, the Steinbergs must have finished ahead of the Stahls, so must have finished in fourth place, and the Stahls finished in fifth place. However, from statement 5, which would be false, the Stanfords must have finished in fourth or fifth place. Therefore, the Steinbergs did not finish in fourth place. Therefore, statement 1 is false; the Steinbergs were either one of the two couples who tied for first place or the couple who finished in third place.

Assume that statement 2 is true. If so, the Stanfords finished in third place. However, from statement 5, which would be false, the Stanfords must have finished in fourth or fifth place. Therefore, statement 2 is false; the Stanfords did not finish in third place.

Assume that statement 3 is the true statement. If so, the Stewarts finished ahead of the Smiths and behind the Stanfords. If so, from statement 5, which would be false, the Stanfords must have finished in fourth place and the Stewarts in fifth place. However, this leaves no place for the Smiths. Therefore, statement 3 is false; the Stewarts finished ahead of the Stanfords and behind the Smiths.

Assume that statement 5 is true. If so, the Stanfords did not finish in either fourth place or fifth place. However, from statement 2, which is false, the Stanfords did not finish in third place; and from what we know from statement 3, the Stewarts finished ahead of the Stanfords and behind the Smiths. Therefore, statement 5 is false.

Assume that statement 6 is true. If so, the Stahls

finished ahead of the Steinbergs and the Smiths. However, from statement 3, which we know is false, the Stanfords must have finished behind both the Stewarts and the Smiths. However, the two who tied for first place must have been two of the Steinbergs, the Smiths, and the Stahls. Therefore, the Stahls could not have finished ahead of both. Therefore, statement 6 is false.

So statement 4 is the true statement. The Smiths finished in third place and the Stanfords in fifth place. The Stewarts were in fourth place, and the Steinbergs and Stahls tied for first place.

SUMMARY SOLUTION

1st place   Steinbergs and Stahls (tied)
3rd place   Smiths
4th place   Stewarts
5th place   Stanfords

S3-40c Jazz Combo

CONSIDERATIONS

Only one statement is true.

Assume statement 1 is true. If so, Caroline is the tenor sax player. From statement 6, which would be false, Roger or Al plays the sax. Therefore, statement 1 is false; Caroline doesn't play the sax.

Assume that statement 2 is true. If so, Steve does not play the piano or the bass. If not, he must play the drums, the guitar, or the sax. From statement 3, which would be false, Steve is not the guitar player. From statement 6, Steve doesn't play the sax. From statement 7, Steve doesn't play the drums. Therefore, statement 2 is false.

Assume statement 4 is the true one. If so, Ansel does not play the guitar, piano, or bass. If not, he must play the sax or the drums. From statement 6, which would be false, he doesn't play the sax, and from statement 7, he doesn't play the drums. Therefore, statement 4 is not the true statement.

Assume statement 5 is the true statement. If so, the drums are not played by Caroline, Ansel, or Roger. If not, the drums are played by Steve or Al. From statement 7, which would be false, the drums are not played by Steve or Al. Therefore, statement 5 is false.

Assume that statement 6 is the true statement. If so, the sax is not played by Roger or Al. If not, the sax must be played by Ansel or Steve (since we know that Caroline doesn't play the sax). From statement 2, which is false, Steve plays the piano or the bass. From statement 4, which is false, Ansel plays the guitar, the piano, or the bass. Therefore, statement 6 is false.

Assume that statement 7 is the true statement. If so, the drums are played by Steve, Ansel, or Al. However, from statement 2, which is false, Steve plays the piano or the bass. From statement 4, which is false, Ansel's instrument is the guitar, the piano, or the bass. From statement 3, which would be false, Al plays the guitar and Ansel plays the piano. Therefore, statement 7 is false.

Therefore, statement 3 is the true statement. The guitar is played by Roger or Steve. From statement 2, Steve plays the piano or the bass. Therefore, Roger plays the guitar. From statement 4, Ansel plays the piano or the bass. From statement 3, Ansel doesn't play the piano. Therefore, he plays the bass. Therefore, Steve plays the piano. From statement 6, Al plays the sax. Therefore, Caroline plays the drums.

SUMMARY SOLUTION

Ansel	bass
Caroline	drums
Al	sax
Roger	guitar
Steve	piano

4. Hyperborea

S4-1 Which Road to Take

CONSIDERATIONS

One is a Sororean and one is a Nororean.

Assume that A is the Sororean, who always speaks truthfully. If so, he truthfully answered Apollo's first inquiry and the road to the left is the one to take. However, Apollo also asked A how B would respond. If so, A would truthfully say that B, who would respond falsely, would say to take the road to the right.

Therefore, A must be the Nororean, who has answered falsely to both questions. B is the Sororean. Apollo should take the road to the right.

SUMMARY SOLUTION

A. Nororean
B. Sororean

Apollo should take the road to the right.

S4-2 Apollo Goes down the Road

CONSIDERATIONS

A cannot be a Sororean, as his first statement would be false, and Sororeans always speak truthfully. A cannot be a Nororean, as his first statement would be truthful, and Nororeans always speak falsely. Therefore, A is a Midrorean. His first statement is false and second statement is true: neither is a Sororean. B's statements are both false. Therefore, B is a Nororean.

SUMMARY SOLUTION

A. Midrorean
B. Nororean

S4-3 Some Just Like to Be Different

CONSIDERATIONS

A's first statement is true. If he were a Sororean, he would truthfully say so. The statement could not be made by a Nororean. Therefore, A is a Midrorean, and his second statement is false. C is not a Midrorean.

Therefore, C's first statement is true. C is a Sororean. From C's second statement, B is a Nororean.

A. Midrorean
B. Nororean
C. Sororean

S4-4 One Speaks Truthfully

CONSIDERATIONS

One speaker is a Sororean, one is a Nororean, and one is a Midrorean.

Assume that A is the Sororean. If so, A's first statement is true: C is the Nororean. If so, B must be the Midrorean. However, C's first statement is that B is the Midrorean. This would be true—not possible for a Nororean. Therefore, A is not the Sororean.

Assume that C is the Sororean. If so, C's first statement that B is the Midrorean would be true. If so, B's first statement would be false and his second statement, that A is the Nororean, would be true. How-ever, A's second statement, that B is not the Sororean, would be true. Again, this is not possible for a Nororean. Therefore, C is not the Sororean.

Therefore, B is the Sororean. As indicated by B's second statement, A is the Nororean. C is the

Midrorean, whose first statement is false and second statement is true.

SUMMARY SOLUTION

A. Nororean
B. Sororean
C. Midrorean

S4-5 Apollo Makes One Last Try

CONSIDERATIONS

One is Sororean, one Nororean, and one Midrorean.

Assume that A is the Sororean. If so, from A's second statement, B would be the Nororean. Therefore, C would be the Midrorean. But A's first statement contradicts this. Therefore, A is not the Sororean.

Assume that B is the Sororean. If so, from B's second statement, C is the Midrorean. This makes A the Nororean. However, from A's third statement, which would be true, A could not be the Nororean. Therefore, C must be the Sororean. B is the Nororean, and A is the Midrorean. A's first and third statements are false and second statement is true.

A. Midrorean
B. Nororean
C. Sororean

S4-6 Who Extracts the Sunflower Seeds?

CONSIDERATIONS

None is a Sororean.

From B's second statement, he is a Midrorean who has spoken falsely (a Nororean could not make that true statement). Therefore, B's first statement is true: A is the olive processor.

A's first statement, that he is the sunflower-seed extractor, is false. Therefore, his third statement is also false. B is the shepherd. By his second statement, C is the sunflower-seed extractor. His first statement is false. Therefore, he is a Midrorean.

A's second statement is false. He is a Nororean.

SUMMARY SOLUTION

A. Nororean   olive processor
B. Midrorean   shepherd
C. Midrorean   sunflower-seed extractor

S4-7 The Delegation of Centaurs

CONSIDERATIONS

One is a Sororean, one is a Nororean, and one is a Midrorean.

Assume that A is the Sororean. If so, from A's two statements, B is the Midrorean and C is the Nororean. However, from C's first statement, which would be true, C could not be the Nororean. Therefore, A is not the Sororean.

Assume that B is the Sororean. If so, from B's statements, again, C would be the Nororean, which is not possible.

Therefore, C is the Sororean. Both of B's statements are false; B is the Nororean. A, whose first statement is true and second statement is false, is the Midrorean.

SUMMARY SOLUTION

A. Midrorean
B. Nororean
C. Sororean

S4-8 The Story of Pelops

CONSIDERATIONS

Consider that one is a Sororean, two are Nororeans, and one is a Midrorean.

A's first statement is false, as Pelops was a visitor from Greece. Assume that A is one of the two Nororeans. If so, from A's second statement, which would be false, C is the second Nororean. However, C's second statement disputes B's first statement, which is false. C's second statement is true, and, therefore, his first statement that he is not a Nororean is also true. Therefore, C is the Sororean and A is not a Nororean. Therefore, A is the Midrorean. B and D are the two Nororeans.

SUMMARY SOLUTION

A. Midrorean
B. Nororean
C. Sororean
D. Nororean

S4-9 Who's Older?

CONSIDERATIONS

Consider that one is a Sororean and three are Midroreans.

Consider A's statements. If A is a Sororean as he claims, A's statements are all true. If A is a Midrorean, his second statement is false, and his first and third statements are true. Therefore, A is the oldest and C is the youngest or second youngest. C, whose first statement claims that he is the oldest, is false. Therefore, he is one of the three Midroreans, and his second statement indicating that B is 100 years older than D is true. So A is 400 years old, B is 300 years old, D is 200 years old, and C is 100 years old.

D's first statement is true, as it confirms what we know, that C is not older than A. However, his second statement claiming that he is older than B is false. D is a Midrorean.

Both of B's statements are true. Therefore, B is the Sororean and A is the third Midrorean.

SUMMARY SOLUTION

A. Midrorean   400 years old
B. Sororean   300 years old

C. Midrorean   100 years old
D. Midrorean   200 years old

S4-10 The Game of Golf

CONSIDERATIONS

At least one is a Nororean.

B's third statement confirms A's third statement. If true, they are both true, and C must be a Nororean. However, if so, C's second statement that he is not a Midrorean would be true. This is not possible for a Nororean. Therefore, C is not a Nororean. Therefore, A's and B's third statements are both false. Therefore, their first statements are both false. B's second statement inferring that he is a Sororean is false. B is a Nororean.

C's first statement disputes B's first statement, which is false. Therefore, C's first statement is true. C's fourth statement contradicts A's first statement, which is false. Therefore, since C's first and fourth statements are true, his second and third statements must also be true. C is a Sororean. From C's third statement, one of the three speakers is a Midrorean. It must be A, whose second statement is true.

A. Midrorean
B. Nororean
C. Sororean

S4-11 Sunflowers Galore

CONSIDERATIONS

The group or groups to which the four speakers belong
are unknown.

A's and B's first statements are both true. B's second statement is false, as we know there are only three
groups, and there are four speakers. Therefore, B is a
Midrorean.

A's second statement must be false. If it were true,
it would be a contradiction, as A would be a Sororean
and we know B to be a Midrorean. Therefore, A is a
Midrorean.

C's first statement is false, as the valuableness of
sunflowers to the inhabitants is a given. C's second
statement, which agrees with A's false second statement, is also false. Therefore, C is a Nororean.

D's first statement, agreeing with B's second statement, which is false, is also false. D's second statement is also false. D is a Nororean.

SUMMARY SOLUTION

A. Midrorean
B. Midrorean
C. Nororean
D. Nororean

S4-12 Who's an Outlier?

CONSIDERATIONS

Consider that one is a Sororean; one is a Nororean; one is a Midrorean; and one is an Outlier.

If B's second statement is true, A is the Sororean, and, as A's first statement indicates, B is the Outlier. If so, B's first statement, denying that he is the Outlier, is false. If so, his third statement is true. However, his third statement disputes A's second statement. Therefore, A is not the Sororean.

Since B claims that A is the Sororean, B is not the Sororean. C, who claims to be the Outlier, is not the Sororean. Therefore, D is the Sororean.

From D's first statement, which is true, B is not the

Outlier. From D's second statement, A's third statement is true. Therefore, A, whose first statement is false and third statement is true, is the Outlier.

B, whose first statement is true and second statement is false, is the Midrorean. B's third statement is true. A's second statement is false.

Therefore, C is the Nororean, whose statements are all false.

SUMMARY SOLUTION

A. Outlier
B. Midrorean
C. Nororean
D. Sororean

S4-13 Who's Grumbling?

CONSIDERATIONS

Consider that only one is a Midrorean; only one is an Outlier; and, as to the other two, little is known.

B's first statement is contradicted by C's third statement. B's first statement is false, and C's third statement is true. B's third statement is false, as it would be true only if B were a Nororean, and a true statement would not be possible for a Nororean. B's second statement and A's first statement are contradictory. One is true and one is false. However, if B's second statement were false, B would have three false statements and B would be a Nororean. However, we know from B's third statement that B is not a Nororean. Therefore, B's second statement is true. B is the Midrorean.

We know that A's first statement is false, since it disagrees with B's second statement, which we know to be true. If A's third statement were false, A would be the Midrorean, but B is the Midrorean. Therefore, A's third statement is true; A is the Outlier.

We know C's third statement to be true; C's second statement agrees with B's second statement, which is true; and C's first statement, that A is not Midrorean, is true. C is a Sororean.

D's first statement, that C is not the Outlier, is true. D's third statement must be true. Since there is only one Midrorean, D's second statement must be true, too. Therefore, D is a Sororean.

SUMMARY SOLUTION

A. Outlier
B. Midrorean
C. Sororean
D. Sororean

S4-14 The Hunt for an Aspidochelon

CONSIDERATIONS

Consider that one is a Midrorean, two are Nororeans, and one is an Outlier.

B's first two statements are false, as it was a given that no one has ever seen an aspidochelon. If B's third statement is true, B is the Outlier; if it is false, B is one of the two Nororeans.

It was a given that the four fishermen are big and husky. Therefore, A's third statement is false. If A's first statement is true, he is the Outlier. If so, B's third statement is also true and B is an Outlier. However, only one of the four is an Outlier. Therefore, A's first statement is false; A is either the Midrorean or one of the two Nororeans; and B, whose third statement is false, is one of the Nororeans.

D's first statement is true and second statement is false. If D's third statement is true, he is the Midrorean; if it is false, he is the Outlier. However, if D's third statement is true, C's third statement is false, which contradicts A's second statement, which makes A's second statement true, and A is a Midrorean. However, there is only one Midrorean. Therefore, D's third statement must be false; D is the Outlier. C's third statement is true, and C's first statement must be true. We know C's second statement to be false; C is the Midrorean. A, whose second statement is false, is the second Nororean.

SUMMARY SOLUTION

A. Nororean
B. Nororean
C. Midrorean
D. Outlier

S4-15 Return from the Aspidochelon Hunt

CONSIDERATIONS

One is a Midrorean, two are Nororeans, and one is an Outlier.

C's first statement, that A's second statement is true, must be false; otherwise, C's first statement is a contradiction. Since it is false, so is A's second statement. Therefore, we can conclude that C is not one of the two Nororeans. This is consistent with C's third statement, that he is not a Nororean.

Therefore, since C's first statement is false and third statement is true, C is the Outlier. His second statement could be either true or false at this point.

We know that A's second statement is false. If either his first or third statement is false, then they are both false, and he is one of the two Nororeans. If either his first or third statement is true, then they are both true, and he is the Midrorean.

A's third statement and D's first statement are in agreement. Therefore, since there is only one Midrorean, both statements must be false, as is A's first statement. A is a Nororean.

Since D's first statement is false, so are his third statement and second statement. D is a Nororean.

Therefore, B, whose second statement is false, and first and third statements are true, is the Midrorean. C's second statement is true.

SUMMARY SOLUTION

A. Nororean
B. Midrorean
C. Outlier
D. Nororean

S4-16 Two Outliers

CONSIDERATIONS

One of the speakers is a Sororean; one is a Midrorean;

one is a Nororean; and the other two speakers are Outliers.

E's third statement is true. If E were the Sororean, he would truthfully say so. B's fourth statement is true, as E must be either the Midrorean or one of the two Outliers. C's first statement could be true or false. If true, B is either the Sororean or one of the Outliers. If false, C is the Midrorean and two of C's statements are true. D's fourth statement, that C is not the Nororean, is true. Therefore, B, C, D, and E each have at least one true statement. Therefore, A is the Nororean, with all false statements.

A's second statement, that B is not the Sororean, is false; B is the Sororean, with all true statements. B's second statement, that C's first statement is false, is true; C is the Midrorean. C's first and third statements are false, and second and fourth statements are true. D and E are the two Outliers.

A's third statement is false: D won the gold medal. B's first statement is true: E won the silver medal. C's third statement, that B did not win the bronze medal, is false: B won the bronze medal.

D's first and fourth statements are true, and second and third statements are false. E's second and third statements are true, and first and fourth statements are false.

445

A. Nororean
B. Sororean, bronze medal winner
C. Midrorean
D. Outlier, gold medal winner
E   Outlier, silver medal winner

S4-17 Apollo Meets an Outlier

CONSIDERATIONS

One and only one is an Outlier and one and only one is a Sororean. As to the other two, little is known.

A's first statement is false; there's only one Outlier. Consider A's second statement. If it is true, B is the Sororean. However, from B's third statement, if true, D is a Sororean, and, therefore, B must not be a Sororean. If B's first statement is false, again, B is not a Sororean. Therefore, A's second statement is false. At this point we can say that A is either a Nororean or the Outlier, and B is not the Sororean.

B's second statement, which confirms A's false first statement, is false. If B's first statement is false, B is a Nororean; if true, B must be the Outlier. Therefore, either A and B are both Nororeans or one is a Nororean and the other is the Outlier.

Assume that A is the Outlier. If so, A's fourth statement, which confirms B's third statement indicating that C is the Outlier, must be false. As to A's third statement, it is disputed by D's fourth statement, which could be true or false.

C's third statement is true, as it disputes B's second statement, which is false. C's second statement, claiming to be the Outlier, must be false. This must be the case, as, if C is the Outlier, B's fourth statement, that A is not the Outlier, is true, making B an Outlier.

Since we know there is only one Outlier, C is not an Outlier. Therefore, C must be a Midrorean.

C's first and third statements are true, and second and fourth statements are false. Therefore, D is a Sororean. D's fourth statement, disputing A's third statement, is true. A is a Nororean. B, whose first and fourth statements are true, and second and third statements are false, is the Outlier.

SUMMARY SOLUTION

A. Nororean
B. Outlier
C. Midrorean
D. Sororean

5. Letters for Digits

S5-1a Subtraction, Three Digits

CONSIDERATIONS

The digits are 0, 4, and 8.

$$
\begin{array}{r}
\text{(3) (2) (1)} \\
\text{A C A} \\
- \ \underline{\text{C C C}} \\
\text{C B C}
\end{array}
$$

From column (2), B must be 0. This leaves 4 and 8 available. Therefore, from columns (1) and (3), A must be 8 and C is 4.

SUMMARY SOLUTION

A B C
8 0 4

```
    8 4 8
-   4 4 4
    4 0 4
```

S5-2a Addition, Four Digits

CONSIDERATIONS

The digits are 1, 2, 3, and 4.

```
  (2) (1)
   A   A
+  B   C
   C   D
```

Given the available digits, since A plus B equals C, column (2), C must be 3. C could not be 4, as, from column (1), D would have to be larger than 4 (no larger digit is available). Therefore, A is 1, D is 4, and B is 2.

SUMMARY SOLUTION

A B C D
1 2 3 4

$$\begin{array}{r} 1\ \ 1 \\ +\ 2\ \ 3 \\ \hline 3\ \ 4 \end{array}$$

S5-3a Subtraction, Four Digits

CONSIDERATIONS

The digits are 2, 4, 6, and 8.

$$\begin{array}{r} (3)\ (2)\ (1) \\ A\ \ B\ \ C \\ -\ B\ \ D\ \ D \\ \hline D\ \ D\ \ B \end{array}$$

From columns (2) and (3), B minus D equals D, and A minus B equals D. Considering the available digits, the only possibility for D is 2. If D were 4, B would be 8, and this won't work for B in column (3) or column (1). Therefore, B equals 4 and A must be 6. C is the remaining digit, 8.

SUMMARY SOLUTION

A B C D
6 4 8 2

```
    6 4 8
  - 4 2 4
    2 2 4
```

S5-4a Addition, Five Digits

CONSIDERATIONS

The digits are 1, 2, 3, 4, and 5.

```
  (3) (2) (1)
    A   A   E
  + E   A   C
    B   D   D
```

From columns (1) and (2), given the available digits, the only possibility for D is 4. Therefore, from column (2), A equals 2. From column (3), B must be 5, and E equals 3. Therefore, C is 1.

SUMMARY SOLUTION

A B C D
2 5 1 4

```
    2 2 3
  + 3 2 1
    5 4 4
```

S5-5a Addition, Six Digits

CONSIDERATIONS

The digits are 0, 2, 3, 4, 5, and 6.

$$
\begin{array}{c}
\text{(5) (4) (3) (2) (1)} \\
\text{A E A C A} \\
+\ \text{E E A B D} \\
\hline
\text{F C D C C}
\end{array}
$$

From column (2), B is 0, since C plus B equals C. From columns (3) and (4), A plus A equals 4 or 6, and E equals 2 or 3. E plus E must equal 4 or 6. Therefore, F, column (4), must equal 5. From column (1), A plus D equals C. Therefore, A must equal 2, D equals 4, and C equals 6.

SUMMARY SOLUTION

A B C D E F
2 0 6 4 3 5

$$
\begin{array}{c}
2\ 3\ 2\ 6\ 2 \\
+\ 3\ 3\ 2\ 0\ 4 \\
\hline
5\ 6\ 4\ 6\ 6
\end{array}
$$

S5-6a Addition, Six Digits Again

CONSIDERATIONS

The digits are 0, 1, 3, 5, 7, and 9.

$$\begin{array}{r} (5)\,(4)\,(3)\,(2)\,(1) \\ B\ C\ E\ C \\ +\ E\ C\ E\ F \\ \hline A\ E\ E\ A\ D \end{array}$$

From column (5), A must be a carry of 1 from column (4). Therefore, from column (2), E must be 5— 5 + 5 + a carry of 1 from column (1). From column (3), C must be 7 considering a carry of 1 from column (2). From column (4), B + 5 + a carry of 1 from column (3) is 15. Therefore, B is 9. From column (1), F is 3 and D is 0.

SUMMARY SOLUTION

A B C D E F
1 9 7 0 5 3

$$\begin{array}{r} 9\ 7\ 5\ 7 \\ +\ 5\ 7\ 5\ 3 \\ \hline 1\ 5\ 5\ 1\ 0 \end{array}$$

S5-7a Subtraction, Five Digits

CONSIDERATIONS

The digits are 2, 3, 5, 7, and 9.

```
      (3) (2) (1)
       A   C   E
   −   C   E   D
       F   F   F
```

From columns (1), (2), and (3), considering the available digits, 2 is the only digit that could represent F in all three columns. From column (1), E minus D must be 9 minus 7, 7 minus 5, or 5 minus 3.

From column (2), C minus E equals 2. Therefore, E cannot be 9. If E is 7, C must be 9. However, from column (3), C cannot be 9. Therefore, from column (1), E is 5 and D is 3. From column (2), C is 7. The remaining letter, A, is 9.

SUMMARY SOLUTION

A C D E F
9 7 3 5 2

$$\begin{array}{r} 9\ 7\ 5 \\ -\ 7\ 5\ 3 \\ \hline 2\ 2\ 2 \end{array}$$

S5-8a Addition, Eight Digits

CONSIDERATIONS

The digits are 0, 1, 2, 3, 4, 5, 6, and 7.

```
(5) (4) (3) (2) 1)
  C   D   A   F   C
+ C   D   C   B   H
  H   E   C   E   G   F
```

C, column (5), must be 5, 6, or 7, since there is a carry in the answer to C plus C, and H, which represents the carry, must be 1. Since we know that H equals 1, F, the sum of C plus H, column (1), must equal one more than C. Therefore, F must equal 7 or 6 and C must equal 5 or 6. A, column (3), must be 1 less than C, since the sum of A plus C plus a possible carry equals C plus C plus a possible carry, column (5). D, column (4), must be 2 or 3, since the sum of D plus D plus possibly a carry from column 3 equals C.

If C is 6, A is 5, F is 7, and D is 3. However, from column (3), A plus C would require a carry to column (4), which would make C 7. Therefore, C must be 5, A is 4, and F is 6. Therefore, E is 0—the sum of C plus C, column (5). D is 2. The two remaining letters, B and G, are 7 and 3 respectively, since, from column (2), F (6) plus B (7) equals G (3) plus a carry to column (4).

SUMMARY SOLUTION

A B C D E F G H
4 7 5 2 0 6 3 1

```
    5 2 4 6 5
  + 5 2 5 7 1
  ----------
  1 0 5 0 3 6
```

S5-9a Addition, Eight Digits Again

CONSIDERATIONS

The digits are 2, 3, 4, 5, 6, 7, 8, and 9.

```
  (5) (4) (3) (2) (1)
           B  C
     E  E  F  E  C
     E  H  D  H  A
  +  H  E  A  E  H
     F  G  G  B  H
```

From columns (5) and (4), F is 7 or 8, E is 2 or 3, and H is 2 or 3. No other possibilities exist without a carry to a sixth column.

From column (4), G is 8 or 9. Therefore, from column (1), given the available digits, C plus C plus A must equal 20. Therefore, there is a carry of 2 to column (2), making the total of 10 for the two E's and one H plus the carry of 2 from column (1). Therefore, from columns (5) and (4), E is 3, H is 2, F is 8, and G is 9. From column (3), D plus A equals ten plus a carry of one from column (2). Therefore, D is 6 or 4, and A is 6 or 4. From column (1), C must be 7, and A is 6. Therefore, D is 4. By elimination, B is 5.

SUMMARY SOLUTION

A B C D E F G H
6 5 7 4 3 8 9 2

```
            5 7
      3 3 8 3 7
      3 2 4 2 6
  +   2 3 6 3 2
      8 9 9 5 2
```

S5-10a Addition, Seven Digits

CONSIDERATIONS

The digits are 1, 2, 3, 4, 5, 7, and 8.

```
(7) (6) (5) (4) (3) (2) (1)
     G   D   B   E   G   A
     D   D   F   B   A   A
 +   D   G   C   B   A   A
 A   E   G   A   B   C   G
```

Column (7) represents a carry from column (6). A

must be 1 or 2. From column (1), A is 1 and G is 3, since no digit is available for G if A were 2.

From columns (5) and (6), since the sums of D, D, and G are different for the two columns, column (5) includes a carry of two from column (4), and column (6) represents a carry of one from column (4). B plus F plus a carry must equal 16. Therefore, B is 7 or 8.

From column (3), B must be 8, as 7 will not work. Therefore, E is 2 and F is 7. From column (2), C is 5. From column (2), F is 7, and from column (5), D is 4.

SUMMARY SOLUTION

A B C D E F G
1 8 5 4 2 763

```
      3 4 8 2 3 1
      4 4 7 8 1 1
    + 4 3 5 8 1 1
    ─────────────
    1 2 3 1 8 5 3
```

S5-11b Subtraction, Four Digits Again

CONSIDERATIONS

The digits are 0, 1, 2, and 3.

```
      (3) (2) (1)
       B   B   A
   −   A   C   A
       A   B   C
```

From columns (1) and (2), C below the line is 0. Therefore, C above the line is 1. Given the available digits, B above is 3, and B below is 2; A above is 2 and A below is 1.

SUMMARY SOLUTION

```
 A B C
 2 3 1
 1 2 0
```

```
     3 2 2
 −   2 1 2
     1 1 0
```

S5-12b Addition, Five Digits Again

CONSIDERATIONS

The digits are 2, 3, 5, 6, and 7.

```
      (4) (3) (2) (1)
       D   D   B   E
    +  E   A   E   B
       C   B   D   A
```

In column (1), E plus B equals A, and in column (2), E plus B equals D. Therefore, there's a carry of 1 from column (1).

The only possibility that works is that A below the line must be 2 and D below the line must be 3. Therefore, D above the line must be 2, and A above must be 3. Therefore, B below is 6, and B above is 5 or 7.

If B above is 5, then E above is 7. However, if so, from column (4), C must be 9. However, the problem does not contain a 9. Therefore, B above is 7; E above is 5; and C is 7.

SUMMARY SOLUTION

```
A B C D
3 7   2
2 6 7 3
```

```
      2 2 7 5
   +  5 3 5 7
      7 6 3 2
```

S5-13b Subtraction, Five Digits Again

CONSIDERATIONS

The digits are 0, 1, 2, 3, and 5.

$$
\begin{array}{cccc}
(4) & (3) & (2) & (1) \\
A & A & D & A \\
- \ E & E & C & E \\
\hline
D & B & F & D \\
\end{array}
$$

Since A minus E is different in column (3) than in column (1), column (3) requires a carry from column (2). Therefore, C is larger than D.

Given the available digits, C must be 5 and D above the line must be 0. D below is 1. F, which is below, is also 5. The remaining digits are 2 and 3. Therefore A, which is larger than E, is 3, and E is 2. B below the line is 0.

SUMMARY SOLUTION

$$
\begin{array}{cccccc}
A & B & C & D & E & F \\
3 & & 5 & 0 & 2 & \\
\hline
2 & 0 & & 1 & 3 & 5 \\
\end{array}
$$

$$
\begin{array}{cccc}
3 & 3 & 0 & 3 \\
- \ 2 & 2 & 5 & 2 \\
\hline
1 & 0 & 5 & 1 \\
\end{array}
$$

S5-14b Addition, Seven Digits Again

CONSIDERATIONS

The digits are 0, 1, 2, 4, 6, 7, and 8.

```
(5) (4) (3) (2) (1)
      A  D  A  E
      F  C  D  E
   +  A  D  E  E
   ─────────────────
   E  F  D  C  F
```

E below, column (5), is a carry from column (4). Therefore, it must be 1 or 2. If it is 2, E above must be 1 (no 3 is available). If so, from column (1), F below the line would have to be 3, which is not available. Therefore, E below is 1, making E above either 0 or 2, making F below either 0 or 6.

However, from column (4), if F is 0, no combination of available numbers could result in a carry of 1 to column (5). Therefore, E above is 2; F below is 6, and F above must be 7. Therefore, A must be 4, anticipating a carry from column (3). The remaining digits are 1 and 8 above, and 0 and 7 below.

Therefore, D is 0 below and 1 above, and C is 8 above and 7 below.

SUMMARY SOLUTION

```
A C D E F
4 8 1 2 7
  7 0 1 6
```

```
    4 1 4 2
    7 8 1 2
  + 4 1 2 2
  1 6 0 7 6
```

S5-15b Addition, Seven Digits Once Again

CONSIDERATIONS

The digits are 0, 1, 2, 3, 4, 5, and 9.

```
(6) (5) (4) (3) (2) (1)
      E   E   C   C   C
  E   E   E   E   F   E
+ E   E   E   D   B   D
A B F A B A
```

From column (6), there is no carry to a seventh column. Therefore, E above the line must be 1, 2, or 4. From columns (4) and (5), the sums of three E's are different in the two columns. This is not the case between the sums in columns (1) and (3). Therefore, it appears that the sum of the three E's in column (4) exceeds ten, providing a carry to column (5). The only alternative would be if E equals 1, F below equals 4, and B below equals 3. However, from column (2), no combination of available digits could equal B below the line. Therefore, E must be 4. Therefore, A is 9, F below is 2, and B below is 3. Of the remaining letters, C is 0, F above is 1, B above is 2, and D is 5.

SUMMARY SOLUTION

```
A B C D E F
  2 0 5 4 1
9 3       2
```

```
    4 4 0 0 0
    4 4 4 4 1 4
+   4 4 4 5 2 5
    9 3 2 9 3 9
```

S5-16c Subtraction, Three Unknown Digits

CONSIDERATIONS

```
  A B
- A A
  A B
```

A below the line must be 0. Therefore, A above is 1. Given that there are 3 digits, B above must be 2, and B below is 1.

SUMMARY SOLUTION

```
A B          1 2
1 2       -  1 1
0 1          0 1
```

S5-17c Subtraction, Four Unknown Digits

CONSIDERATIONS

```
  (5) (4) (3) (2) (1)
   A  B  A  A  C
-  A  C  C  A  A
   A  A  B  C
```

From column (2), B below the line must be 0 or 9, depending on whether or not there is a carry to column (1). Assume B below is 0. If so, B above is 1. If so, since there is no carry from column (5), C above in column (4) must be 0. However, from column (1), if C above is 0, there must be a carry from column (2). Therefore, B below is not 0; it is 9. Therefore, B above is 8.

In column (1), C above equals C below plus 1 or C below equals minus 1. If C above equals C below plus 1, then A above equals 1. If C above equals C below minus 1, then A above equals 9. However, if A above equals 1, there's no carry from column (1), since C cannot equal 0 above and 9 below. Therefore, A above equals 9 and A below equals 8. Therefore, C above must be 0, and C below is one.

SUMMARY SOLUTION

```
A B C
9 8 0
8 9 1
```

```
  9 8 9 9 0
- 9 0 0 9 9
  8 8 9 1
```

S5-18c Addition, Five Unknown Digits

CONSIDERATIONS

$$
\begin{array}{r}
(4)\,(3)\,(2)\,(1) \\
A \ C \ D \ A \\
+ \ A \ C \ A \ A \\
\hline
C \ B \ A \ C
\end{array}
$$

From column (4), A above the line must be a digit less than 5, since there is no carry to a 5th column. Since column (4) is the same as column (1), there is no carry from column (3) to column (4). So A above the line can only be 1 or 2. If A above the line is 1, C below is 2 and C above must be 3. A below must be 0 and D above would be 9. That's already 5 digits, but we haven't accounted for B. Therefore, A above is 2, and C below is 4. C above must be 3, since column (4) has no carry. A below is 1 or 3. But if it is 1, D above is 9, and that is five digits without accounting for B. So A below is 3, D is 1, and B is 6.

SUMMARY SOLUTION

$$
\begin{array}{llll}
A & B & C & D \\
2 & & & 1 \\
\hline
3 & 6 & 4 &
\end{array}
$$

```
      2 3 1 2
  +   2 3 2 2
    ─────────
      4 6 3 4
```

S5-19c Addition, Five Unknown Digits Again

CONSIDERATIONS

```
    (5) (4) (3) (2) (1)
     A   D   A   B   A
  +  C   A   C   B   A
    ──────────────────
     D   B   A   B   C
```

From column (3), C above the line must represent 0, 1, or 9, depending on whether or not there is a carry from column (2). But there is no carry from column (5), so C above is not 9.

From column (2), B above the line must represent 0, 1, or 9. If B above is 9, C above must be 0. Otherwise, A below the line could not be one number different from A above the line. However, if C above the line is 0, C below the line must be 1, and, from column (1), no number represented by A plus A could equal 1 or 11.

Therefore, C above the line is 1, and C below is 0 or 2 depending on whether A above is 5 or 6. Since there is a carry to column (2), B above the line is 0, and B below the line is 1. (If B above is 9, B below would have to be 9; if B above is 1, B below would have to be 3, neither of which is possible.)

From column (4), D above plus A above equals 1 and a carry to column (5). Since A is either 5 or 6, D must be 6 or 5. From column (5), since A above plus C above plus a carry of 1 equals D below, A above must be 5, D below is 7, and D above is 6.

From column (3), A below is 6, and from column (1), C below is 0.

SUMMARY SOLUTION

```
A B C D
5 0 1 6
6 1 0 7
```

```
    5 6 5 0 5
  + 1 5 1 0 5
    7 1 6 1 0
```

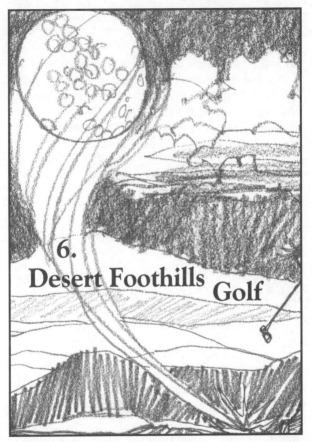

6.
Desert Foothills Golf

S6-1 The First Decision

CONSIDERATIONS

Consider that at least one of the signs is false.

Assume that path A is the path to take. If so, sign A is true. However, since at least one of the signs is false, sign B would have to be false. There is no way to validate sign B as being false. Therefore, sign A is false, as is sign B. Path B is the path to take.

	sign A	sign B
If path A	T	T
If path B	F	F

SUMMARY SOLUTION

Path B is correct.

S6-2 The Second Decision

CONSIDERATIONS

Consider that the correct decision can conclusively be made.

Assume that path B is the correct path. If so, sign B is true and sign C is false. However, it is impossible to decide conclusively whether sign A is true or false. If it is true, it is false; if it is false, it is true. The same conclusion must be drawn if the assumption is made that path C is the one to take. Therefore, path A is the one to take.

	sign A	sign B	sign C
If path A	T	F	F
If path B	T/F	T	F
If path C	T/F	F	T

SUMMARY SOLUTION

Path A is the correct path.

S6-3 The Third Decision

CONSIDERATIONS

Consider that only one of the signs is true.

Assume that path A is the correct choice. If so, the sign at path A is true; the sign at path B is false; and the sign at path C is true. Therefore, path A is not the right choice. Assume that path B is the right one. If so, the sign at path A is false, and the signs at paths B and C are both true. Therefore, path C is correct: the sign at path A is true and the signs at paths B and C are both false.

	sign A	sign B	sign C
If path A	T	F	T
If path B	F	T	T
If path C	T	F	F

SUMMARY SOLUTION

Take path C.

S6-4 The Fourth Decision

CONSIDERATIONS

Consider that at least one sign is false.

Assume that path B is correct. If so, all three signs are true. Assume that path C is the right path. Again, if so, all three signs are true. Therefore, path A is the correct path. All three signs are false.

	sign A	sign B	sign C
If path A	F	F	F
If path B	T	T	T
If path C	T	T	T

SUMMARY SOLUTION

Path A is the right path.

S6-5 The Fifth Decision

CONSIDERATIONS

Consider that exactly one of the signs is false.

Assume that path A is the correct path. If so, the sign at path A is false, as is the sign at path B. (The sign at path C can be true or false, but that's immaterial, since there are already two false signs.) Therefore, path A is not the way to go. Assume that path C is right. If so, the sign at path A is true.

However, the signs at paths B and C are both false. Therefore, path B is the correct path: the sign at path A is false and the signs at paths B and C must both be true.

	sign A	sign B	sign C
If path A	F	F	T/F
If path B	F	T	T
If path C	T	F	F

SUMMARY SOLUTION

Path B is the one to take.

S6-6 The Sixth Decision

CONSIDERATION

Consider that exactly one sign is false.

Assume that path A is correct. If so, the sign at path A is true. However, the signs at paths B and C are both false. Therefore, path A is not the way to go. Assume that path C is correct. If so, the sign at path A is true, and the signs at paths B and C are both false. Therefore, the path to take is B.

	sign A	sign B	sign C
If path A	T	F	F
If path B	F	T	T
If path C	T	F	F

SUMMARY SOLUTION

Path B is the correct path.

S6-7 The Seventh Decision

CONSIDERATIONS

Consider that the sign at the path to take is the only false one.

If path B is the correct path, the sign at path B is false. But then the sign at path C cannot be true, since only one sign is false. So path B is not correct.

If path C is the correct path, the sign at path C is false and the sign at path A must be true. But this is impossible. So path C is not the correct path. The correct path is path A. The sign at path A is false, the sign at path B is true, and the sign at path C is true.

SUMMARY SOLUTION

	sign A	sign B	sign C
If path A	F	T	T
If path B	T	F	F
If path C	F	T	F

Take path A.

S6-8 The Eighth Decision

CONSIDERATIONS

Consider that one or more signs are false.

Assume that path A is correct. If so, the sign at path A is true, as are the signs B and C. Assume that path C is the right path. If so, all three signs are true. Therefore, B is the correct path: the sign at path A is true, the sign at path B is false, and the sign at path C is true.

	sign A	sign B	sign C
If path A	T	T	T
If path B	T	F	T
If path C	T	T	T

SUMMARY SOLUTION

Path B is the correct path.

S6-9 The Ninth Decision

CONSIDERATIONS

Consider that at least two signs are false.

Assume that path A will lead to the clubhouse. If so, all three signs are true. Therefore, path A is not the way to go. Assume that path B is correct. If so, the sign at path A is false, and the sign at path B is true, as is the sign at path C. Therefore, path C is the way to the clubhouse. All three signs are false.

	sign A	sign B	sign C
If path A	T	T	T
If path B	F	T	T
If path C	F	F	F

SUMMARY SOLUTION

Path C will lead to the clubhouse.

7. Namesakes

S7-1 Four Fishing Boats

CONSIDERATIONS

From statement 2, Jeb's horse is named King. Therefore, King is not the name of his fishing boat.

From statements 3 and 4, Jeb's fishing boat is not named Ace or Beau. Therefore, Jeb's fishing boat is named Spike. Since Joe's fishing boat is named Ace (statement 3), Jake's fishing boat must be named King or Beau.

From statement 1, Jake's fishing boat is named after Jay's horse. Therefore, since Jeb's horse is named King, Jay's horse and Jake's fishing boat are both named Beau.

Therefore, Jay's fishing boat is named King. Since Joe's fishing boat is named Ace, his horse must be named Spike, and Jake's horse is named Ace.

	horse	**boat**
Jake	Ace	Beau
Jay	Beau	King
Jeb	King	Spike
Joe	Spike	Ace

S7-2 Knowheyan Paddlebird Tournament

CONSIDERATIONS

From statement 1, the visitor Larry was not teamed with the inhabitant Lenny. Therefore, the visitor Larry was teamed with either the Knowheyan Logan or Lewis.

From statement 2, the visitor Lenny was not teamed with the Knowheyan Larry. Therefore, the visitor Lenny was teamed with the Knowheyan Logan or Lewis.

From statement 3, the visitor Logan was not teamed with the Knowheyan Lewis. Therefore, the visitor Logan was teamed with either the Knowheyan Larry or Lenny.

From statement 4, the visitor Logan was teamed with the Knowheyan Larry. Therefore, the visitor Larry was teamed with the Knowheyan Lewis, the visitor Lenny was teamed with the Knowheyan Logan, and, by elimination, the visitor Lewis was teamed with the Knowheyan Lenny.

SUMMARY SOLUTION

Visitor Larry	Knowheyan Lewis
Visitor Lenny	Knowheyan Logan
Visitor Logan	Knowheyan Larry
Visitor Lewis	Knowheyan Lenny

S7-3 Burglaries in the Neighborhood

CONSIDERATIONS

From statements 1, 3, and 6, Milton's dog is not named Moriarty, Maurice, Martin, or Marion. Therefore, Milton's dog is named Melville. Therefore, from statement 5, Martin's dog is named Milton, and, from statement 1, Melville's dog is named Moriarty. Therefore, from statement 2, Moriarty owns the dog named Marion.

Therefore, Maurice's dog is named Martin, and Marion's dog is named Maurice. From statement 4, the burglar is Moriarty.

SUMMARY SOLUTION

Marion's dog is Maurice
Martin's dog is Milton
Maurice's dog is Martin
Melville's dog is Moriarity
Milton's dog is Melville
Moriarty's dog is Marion

The burglar is Moriarty.

S7-4 Wine Connoisseurs

CONSIDERATIONS

From statement 3, the Merlots gave or received port and/or sherry and/or chardonnay. From statement 4, the Merlots did not receive port, which must have been received by the Sherrys or the Chardonnays. From statement 1, the Sherrys received merlot. Therefore, the Chardonnays received port and the Merlots received chardonnay.

Therefore, from statement 2, the Ports gave chardonnay and received burgundy. Therefore, from statement 5, the Burgundys gave port. Therefore, the

Merlots gave sherry. From statement 6, the bordeaux was given by the Chardonnays and received by the Burgundys.

Therefore, the Sherrys must have given the burgundy; the Bordeauxs gave the merlot and received the sherry.

SUMMARY SOLUTION

connoisseurs	**gave**	**received**
Bordeauxs	merlot	sherry
Burgundys	port	bordeaux
Chardonnays	bordeaux	port
Merlots	sherry	chardonnay
Ports	chardonnay	burgundy
Sherrys	burgundy	merlot

8. Things in Order

S8-1 Wood-Chopping Contest

SOLUTION

1. Egum
2. Epum
3. Elfum
4. Efrum
5. Ekum
6. Evum
7. Estum
8. Esum
9. Edum
10. Ebum
11. Eskum
12. Ensum

S8-2 Goblins, Ogres, and Giants

SOLUTION

1. Ocho   goblin
2. Veb   goblin
3. Par   ogre
4. Ejo   goblin

5.	Rio	goblin	11.	Geb	goblin
6.	Hab	ogre	12.	Fane	ogre
7.	Deg	goblin	13.	Boe	goblin
8.	Tose	giant	14.	Dino	giant
9.	Bib	ogre	15.	Coj	ogre
10.	Zed	goblin			

S8-3 Trees in the Forest

SOLUTION

	one side of the path	other side of the path
9.	maple	hickory
8.	oak	poplar
7.	elm	ash
6.	willow	tamarack
5.	fir	yew
4.	cedar	spruce
3.	birch	juniper
2.	hemlock	alder
1.	pine	aspen

S8-4 Fishing Flies

SOLUTION

1. Murphy's No. 1
2. Adams
3. Olive Blue Dun
4. Gold Ribbed Hare's Ear
5. Woolly Bugger
6. Maribou Muddler
7. Royal Wulff
8. Grey Wulff
9. Royal Humpy
10. Wright's Royal
11. Elk Hair Caddis
12. Light Cahill
13. Prince Nymph
14. Brook's Stone Fly
15. Zug Bug
16. Joe's Hopper

S8-5 Varieties of Fruit

SOLUTION

Back row: pears, oranges, peaches, plums, cherries, loquats, persimmons, apricots, papayas, guavas.

Front row: limes, watermelons, bananas, blackberries, strawberries, raspberries, lemons, mangos, nectarines, grapes.

S8-6 Chivalrous Knights

SOLUTION

1. Sir Intrepid
2. Sir Valorous
3. Sir Gallant
4. Sir Daring
5. Sir Fearless
6. Sir Faithful
7. Sir Resolute
8. Sir Trustworthy
9. Sir Bold
10. Sir Resourceful
11. Sir Hector
12. Sir Dauntless
13. Sir Loyal
14. Sir Victor
15. Sir Admirable
16. Sir Virtue
17. Sir True
18. Sir Dependable

S8-7 The Tournament Pavilions

SOLUTION

	left to right facing east	right to left facing west
1.	Sir Fearless	Sir Daring
2.	Sir Dauntless	Sir Reliable
3.	Sir True	Sir Victor
4.	Sir Hector	Sir Virtue
5.	Sir Faithful	Sir Gallant
6.	Sir Loyal	Sir Admirable

7.	Sir Able	Sir Valorous
8.	Sir Resolute	Sir Resourceful
9.	Sir Dependable	Sir Bold
10.	Sir Trustworthy	Sir Intrepid

S8-8 Banners of the Winners

The sixteen banners are arranged in a triangle shape as follows:

red and
emerald-
green

silver	burgundy	olive
on	on	on
on black	gray	yellow

cream	sky-blue	red	black	charcoal
on	on	on	on	on
olive	silver	white	white	orange

forest-	copper	yellow	gold	egg-shell	bronze	gold on
green on	on	on nut-	on jade-	blue and	on	royal-
gold	yellow	brown	green	cream	cream	blue

S8-9 New Neighbors

SOLUTION

	left to right **facing east**	right to left **facing west**
1.	Maloneys	Mahoneys
2.	Mayers	Marshalls
3.	Maxwells	Mathesons
4.	Mallettes	Marleaus
5.	Marlows	Martins
6.	Mayburys	Majors
7.	Malones	Magnans
8.	Mastersons	Marquardts
9.	Mallorys	Marsdens
10.	Marshes	Mathews
11.	Mayfields	Matsens
12.	Matlocks	Macklins

S8-10 Devoted to Opera

SOLUTION

1. Manon
2. Tannhauser
3. Don Giovanni
4. Carmen
5. Die Meitersinger
6. Parsifal
7. Cosí Fan Tutte
8. Elektra
9. Arabella
10. Falstaff
11. Rigoletto
12. La Traviata
13. Amahl and the Night Visitors
14. The Bartered Bride
15. Otello
16. Faust
17. Tristan and Isolde
18. Lohengrin
19. Cavalleria Rusticana
20. Don Pasquale
21. Pagliacci
22. Aïda
23. Don Carlos
24. Tosca
25. Boris Godunof
26. La Gioconda
27. La Bohême
28. Peter Grimes
29. Die Fledermaus
30. Madame Butterfly

9. The Dragons of Lidd

S9-1 Two Dragons

CONSIDERATIONS

From A's first statement, he must be a rational. If A were a predator, he would lie and say he was red. He could be a gray rational that has spoken truthfully or a red rational that has lied. Since A's second statement is true, he is a gray rational.

B's first statement is a lie, as we know that A is a rational. Therefore, B's second statement is also a lie. B is a gray predator.

SUMMARY SOLUTION

A. gray rational
B. gray predator

S9-2 Two More Dragons

CONSIDERATIONS

From B's second statement we can determine his type, whether or not he is telling the truth. Both gray and red rationals would claim to be gray; a gray predator would claim to be red, and a red predator would speak the truth. There, B is a gray or red predator.

From A's first statement we can conclude that his statements are false, and from his second statement we can conclude that B's statements are true. A is a gray predator. B is a red predator.

SUMMARY SOLUTION

A. gray predator
B. red predator

S9-3 Three to One

CONSIDERATIONS

Assume that C's second statement, that A is red, is true. If so, from A's first statement, that he is not a predator, he must be a red rational. However, red rationals always lie and red predators always speak the truth. Therefore, C's second statement is false. A is either a gray predator or a gray rational.

From C's first statement, which we know to be false, all three are not rationals. From C's third statement, which is also false, we can conclude that B is gray. This is consistent with A's second statement. Therefore, A has spoken the truth. A is a gray rational.

B's third statement, that A's statements are true, is true. Therefore, B is a gray rational. From C's first statement, which is false, C must be a gray predator.

SUMMARY SOLUTION

A. gray rational
B. gray rational
C. gray predator

S9-4 Three to One Again

CONSIDERATIONS

If either part of a statement is false, the statement is false. Therefore, since rationals do not eat people, A has spoken falsely: he is either a red rational or a gray predator. A's second statement must be false. Therefore, either one or both of B and C are rationals.

C's third statement, that claims that A's second statement is false, is true. Therefore, he is a gray rational, as indicated by his second statement. From C's first statement, A and B are both predators.

From B's statements, which are false, A and B are both gray.

SUMMARY SOLUTION

A. gray predator
B. gray predator
C. gray rational

S9-5 Whose Colors Are the Same?

CONSIDERATIONS

B's second statement is that he is not red. If the statement is true, B must be a gray rational; if it is false, he must be a red rational. Therefore, it is evident that dragon C's first statement is false, as is his second statement: dragon C and dragon A are not the same color.

Therefore, dragon A's second statement is true, as is his first statement. Dragon A is a gray rational; dragon C must be a red rational; and dragon B, whose statements are true, is a gray rational.

SUMMARY SOLUTION

A. gray rational
B. gray rational
C. red rational

S9-6 Three on Three

CONSIDERATIONS

Assume that A's second statement is true. If so, he's a gray rational and B and C are predators. B's second statement would be true, so he would be a red predator. Therefore, from B's first statement, C would be a red predator, too. But then C's second statement would be false, which is impossible. So A's second statement is false; he is not a rational, and, since he lied, he's a gray predator. B's first statement is false, so his second statement is also false. He, too, is a gray predator. Since A's first statement is false, C must be a rational. Since his statements are both true, he's gray.

SUMMARY SOLUTION

A. gray predator
B. gray predator
C. gray rational

S9-7 Are There Any Predators Left?

CONSIDERATIONS

Assume that A's statements are true. If so, B's second statement and A's second statements are true, and C is a red predator. However, if so, C has spoken the truth. From C's first statement, both A and B are predators, which means that B's first statement is false. Therefore, A's statements are false, and from A's first statement, B's statements are also false.

From A's second statement, which is false, C is gray, and from B's second statement, which is false, C is a rational. Therefore, from C's statements, A and B are both gray predators.

SUMMARY SOLUTION

A. gray predator
B. gray predator
C. gray rational

S9-8 How Many Are Rationals?

CONSIDERATIONS

Between B and C, it is clear that one speaks the truth and one lies. Assume that C speaks the truth. If so, since B's third statement is false, A's third statement must be true. If so, from A's first statement, A is a red predator. However, this contradicts C's second statement. Therefore, B speaks the truth and C lies. B is a gray rational. From B's third statement, A lies. From C's first statement, which we know to be false, A would falsely claim to be a predator. Therefore, A is a red rational; and from A's second statement, which we know to be false, C would falsely claim to be gray. Therefore, C is also a red rational.

SUMMARY SOLUTION

A. red rational
B. gray rational
C. red rational

S9-9 Three on Three Again

CONSIDERATIONS

Between A and B, it is apparent from their first statements that one is speaking the truth and one is lying.

Assume that B's statements are true. If so, from B's second statement, C would confirm B's statement. However, C's second statement supports A's first statement. Therefore, B's statements are false. A's statements are true, as are C's statements, as confirmed by A's second statement. A is a red predator, as indicated by C.

From C's first statement, B, whose statements are false, is a gray predator, and C is a gray rational.

SUMMARY SOLUTION

A. red predator
B. gray predator
C. gray rational

The Dragons from Wonk

S9-10 Four Dragons

CONSIDERATIONS

Assume that C's first statement, that he is the only one that speaks the truth, is true. If so. D's first statement must be false. However, if so, from D's first statement, A speaks the truth. Therefore, C's statements are false. From C's second statement, which is false, C is a gray predator.

A's third statement is true. Therefore, from A's second statement, he is a gray rational.

D's first statement, that A does not speak the truth,

is false. From D's second statement, D is a red rational.

From A's first statement, B must be the second dragon that speaks the truth. From B's second statement, he is a red predator.

SUMMARY SOLUTION

A. gray rational
B. red predator
C. gray predator
D. red rational

S9-11 One Is Blue

CONSIDERATIONS

B has given himself away. Only a blue dragon from Wonk could make his first statement. A dragon from the Kingdom of Lidd would have to deny being a red rational or a gray predator. Therefore, from B's second statement, A is a rational, as he claims. Since he has spoken the truth, A is a gray rational and B is a blue predator.

SUMMARY SOLUTION

A. gray rational
B. blue predator

S9-12 Two of Three Are Blue

CONSIDERATIONS

From B's first statement, we can conclude that B is either a gray predator or a red predator. If he were a blue dragon, his statement would be true. Therefore, A and C are the two blue dragons.

From A's statement, that he is a rational, we can conclude that he is a predator. From C's statement, he is a rational.

B's second statement is true. Therefore, B is a red predator.

SUMMARY SOLUTION

A. blue predator
B. red predator
C. blue rational

S9-13 One of Three Is Blue

CONSIDERATIONS

From C's second statement we can conclude that he is not the blue dragon. He is either a red rational or a gray predator.

From C's first statement, which is false, A's first statement is true, B is the blue dragon. From A's second statement, B and C are predators and C is gray. A is a gray rational.

SUMMARY SOLUTION

A. gray rational
B. blue predator
C. gray predator

S9-14 At Least One Is a Blue Dragon

CONSIDERATIONS

From B's second statement, we can conclude that B is not a blue dragon. He is either a red rational or a gray predator. D, whose first statement confirms that B is not blue, has made a true statement. He is either a gray rational or a red predator. Either A or C or both are blue.

B's first statement, that C is a predator, is false. Therefore, C is a rational. C's first statement, that he is a predator, is false. Therefore, C's second statement, that A is not a blue dragon, is false; A is a blue dragon. From A's third statement, that only one is a blue dragon, we can conclude that C is a second blue dragon. D's second statement, that B would state that A is a predator, indicates that A is a rational.

A's second statement, that C would state that D is a predator, is false. C would falsely state that D is a rational. D is a red predator. C's third statement, that three are rationals, is false. Therefore, B must be a gray predator.

SUMMARY SOLUTION

A. blue rational
B. gray predator
C. blue rational
D. red predator

S9-15 How Many Blue Dragons?

CONSIDERATIONS

Assume that A's first statement is true. If so, C's first statement and B's first statements are both true. If so, D's second statement, that A is a rational, must be true, as it is consistent with B's first statement. However, A's second statement, that D is blue, conflicts with our assumption. Therefore, A's statements are false, as are B's and C's statements.

From C's third statement, we can conclude that D's statements are true. From D's second statement, A is a rational, and from D's first statement, B, C, and D are predators.

Since his statements are true, D is a red predator. From D's second statement A is a red rational. From B's and C's second statements, which are false, we can conclude that two, B and C, are blue dragons.

SUMMARY SOLUTION

A. red rational
B. blue predator
C. blue predator
D. red predator

Index

Page key: puzzle, **solution.**

507

About the Author

Norman D. Willis is a retired international management consultant. He lives in Tucson, where he spends much of his time year-round playing golf. This is Mr. Willis's sixth book.